The Creative Homemaker

Mrs. Mary La Grand Bouma

The Creative Homemaker

Mary LaGrand Bouma

bethany
fellowship

MINNEAPOLIS, MINNESOTA

Library of Congress Cataloging in Publication Data

Bouma, Mary La Grand
The Creative Homemaker
1. Home Economics
2. Mothers—Religious Life
3. Wives—Religious Life
I. Title
TX147.B68
640
73-17234
ISBN 0-87123-078-X

Printed in the United States of America

DEDICATION

To Henry—my husband,
theological editor,
mentor, and inspiration.

ACKNOWLEDGEMENTS

A special word of thanks must go to my prayer partners:

Lois Bruizeman
Bretta Chadwick
Greta Foley
Barbara Gocus
Jo Koetje
Kathy Orren
Nancy Piehl
Sue Sausser

who prayed the whole project into being, chapter by chapter. Their faithful support was invaluable.

Also thank you to Jan Blackburn, who managed to type each chapter as I finished it, while caring for her three small children at the same time.

There are many others, too numerous to mention, who helped with their prayers, with typing, or by supplying information. I wish to say a warm "thank you" to all of them.

I am indebted to *Christianity Today* for the use of material which first appeared in my article "Liberated Mothers" in the May 7, 1971 issue of their magazine.

My thanks also to *Bible Studies*, the adult Sunday school paper published by the Board of Publications of the Christian Reformed Church, 2850 Kalamazoo Avenue, Grand Rapids, Michigan, for permission to incorporate in this book parts of several articles which I wrote for them.

Thanks also to the following:

Quotations from the "Today's English Version of the New Testament." Copyright © American Bible Society 1966, 1971. Used by permission.

Contents

Introduction

The institution of the home is threatened more today than perhaps ever before. It faces assault from without and decay from within. Marriage partners, when encountering difficulties and problems, are often simply giving up on the marriage. Divorce has become commonplace. At the same time many of our "advanced" thinkers insist that marriage and the home as we know it are outmoded. They encourage us to experiment with other life-styles more suited to this modern age.

And yet, for the Christian woman it is a wonderful time to be a wife and mother. There are seemingly unlimited opportunities for growing and maturing as a person in Christ and for serving one's family, one's community, and the world. It is true that homemaking is scrubbing floors, washing diapers, and wiping runny noses. But it can be a great deal more! It is potentially the greatest career open to a wife and mother. Checking out groceries or typing sales reports is no more creative than cooking and cleaning. Even such important professions as social work and teaching cannot overshadow home-making as a high calling. Homemaking seen in its broadest sense, and seen from a Biblical perspective, is the most exciting, challenging, and fulfilling career a woman can have. That is what this book is all about.

In a sense this book has been many years in preparation. My husband and I started our ministry fourteen years ago on the prairies of Canada, where a sense of community was strong and marriages stable. Not all couples were living with optimum joy in their marriages, but they did not consider divorce to be an option, nor did they spend time analyzing their marriages to determine whether or not they were successful. Although there were stresses and strains on the family, the members worked as a unit. The home was simply there—breaking up a family was unthinkable.

Four years later we moved to the San Francisco Bay area. This was something of a cultural shock. During that time the divorce rate in the county north of us, where many of our people lived, was higher than the marriage rate. We began to see that the family was really in trouble. There were children coming to Sunday school who were not sure what their last names were. Often a child had had two or three stepfathers and did not know which name he was supposed to use. Our children began to notice what was going on around us. One day on the way home from a visit with one of these families, our five-year-old asked earnestly, "You and Daddy aren't going to get a divorce, too, are you?"

Five years ago, when we moved to our present community, we found the situation to be basically the same. We became involved with a number of people with problem marriages. In our counseling my husband and I both gradually came to see that no matter whose "fault" the poblem is, the woman is in the most important position. She can bring stability to the home and marriage.

We became aware that there were some real difficulties

that no one was dealing with and for which only the Bible has the answer. I began to look carefully at what the Bible has to say about marriage and the family and to read all the books and articles I could find on the subject. I began to reflect on what I was reading and what I saw going on around me. At the same time I was keeping a file.

As I talked these things over with my husband, he kept encouraging me to write, telling me that I could make a positive case for homemaking from a Biblical viewpoint. After writing several articles for various publications and reviewing my file, I realized that I had already completed most of my research. So with my family's encouragement and cooperation, I set about to complete the task.

I am speaking primarily to wives and mothers, so at times what I am saying may appear to be one-sided. This is necessarily so. I do mention some of the implications for husbands and fathers, but do not deal with them at any length. For instance, in the chapter on Child-Raising, I refer particularly to the mother's role, although much of the material applies to both parents. This does not mean that the husband's role in marriage and his responsibilities as a father should be ignored. They are of vital importance. But that would be another book, preferably written by a man.

Mary La Grand Bouma

CHAPTER 1

On Being a Wife

In a recent issue of *The National Enquirer*, sociologist Ersel Le Masters is quoted as saying, "Man is no longer king in his castle. There has been a palace revolution and the father has emerged as the court jester. I grew up in a family where my father was king. I'm sure not king in my family, and I don't know any man who thinks he is king in his." He goes on to say, "The father in contemporary society has become displaced as the dominant parent by the mother."

Nowadays the role of women, particularly married women, is very much discussed. We used to be "just housewives" and largely ignored. Now we are news. But it is not very fashionable to talk about what makes a good wife. On every hand we are urged to fulfill ourselves as persons by finding our identities apart from our husbands. We are told to find careers outside of our homes so that we can mature and reach our potential as persons in our own right. However, we should be aware that this kind of thinking is a product of our individualistic age and runs counter to Biblical teaching and thought. The Bible speaks in terms of community, of fellowship. Man and woman were created to have fellowship with each other; the church is a community of believers. God's people always grow and mature in community.

Husband and Wife Are Complementary

The creation account tells us that woman was made for man. But at the same time it tells us that man was incomplete without woman. Genesis 1:26-27 makes it clear that man and woman together reflect the image of God, and not simply man alone. "And God said, Let us make man in our image, after our likeness. . . . So God created man in his own image . . . male and female created he them." So although the woman's position is different from the man's, she is in no way inferior. Both are equally important in God's scheme of things and each needs the other. The second chapter of Genesis tells us that man was lonely by himself. He was incomplete; so God created woman. As Larry Christenson says in *The Christian Family*, "He didn't just create man. There was something missing. So . . . He created woman. Now He had the whole thing. Man and woman came together in marriage, manifesting God's ideal of completeness." Man and woman complement each other not only physically, but intellectually, emotionally, and spiritually. Since man and woman together reflect the image of God, they will grow and develop their potential best as they grow together. The idea that a man and wife must go their own ways to find fulfillment and maturity as persons is not Biblical.

There are, of course, people whose calling it is to be single. Jesus talks of "eunuchs for the kingdom" in Matthew 19:12. However, He indicates that this is somewhat of an exception. Paul follows through on this thought in I Corinthians 7. He himself is an example of one whose calling was to be celibate to further the cause of the gospel.

Married women, however, have a different calling. Ephesians 5:22-24 says, "Wives, submit yourselves unto your own husbands, as unto the Lord. For the husband is the head of the wife, even as Christ is the head of the church: and he is the saviour of the body. Therefore as the church is subject unto Christ, so let the wives be to their own husbands in everything." As the church finds her destiny in total commitment to Christ, in the same way wives will find their destinies in their husbands. Although the wife's role is not one of leadership, it is not less necessary than the husband's. Submission is a means of strength and power for a woman. As we study the history of the church we see that it has been most gloriously effective, most powerful in its impact when it has been the most submissive to the will of Christ. We sometimes look back to the early years of the church with awe and a certain wistfulness. When the Christians were persecuted and martyred for the faith, the church was the strongest. Why? Because Christians were submitting totally to Christ, to the point of death.

Christ himself made His incomparably glorious sacrifice through submitting to the will of the Father. There is nothing degrading about submission. Submitting to proper, God-ordained authority does not prove one's inferiority. Quite the opposite. It often takes a superior person to submit. This is not an easy thing to do. In fact, it may be the hardest thing that some of us are ever called to do! We may have to go through our own personal Gethsemane before we gain the victory in this matter. All of us, as our first parents did, want to do "our own thing." By nature we want to do exactly what *we* want, not what someone else tells us or suggests.

Women have been trying to take over the leadership of their marriages for centuries, and many of them have succeeded. There are many wives in North America today who have usurped their husbands' position. The results are always disastrous. My husband calls these "upside-down" marriages. The husband is unable to be the head of the wife, she is not submitting, and both of them are miserable. I know many couples with this kind of marriage, and none of them are really happy. The wives seem to suffer the most; they usually sense that things are not the way they should be, and they feel guilty.

It is interesting that the children in these situations are not fooled, even when the marriage partners are fooling themselves. Sometimes the subject comes up in a Sunday school class or in an informal conversation. On more than one occasion a young person has volunteered, "My mom sure is the boss in *our* house." In one discussion of presidents and their wives, a teenager announced, "If my dad were president, my mother would run the country."

In many of these cases I am quite sure the parents have not admitted this to themselves, but the children are not fooled. Children in these situations suffer in many ways. For one thing, during their formative years they are getting the wrong idea of what a family should be. In this way the "sins of the fathers" are often visited on the children in the next generation when they begin to set up their homes. Unless something important occurs to change their direction, their marriages will naturally follow the pattern of the homes in which they grew up.

One couple who came to a Christian psychologist for counseling discovered that their household was in chaos because neither partner was expecting to give leadership. The wife, who came from a home where the father and mother assumed their proper roles, was expecting her husband to lead. He, on the other hand, had been raised in a family where the mother ran things and the father merely brought home the money. This young husband, without thinking about it, was patterning his behavior after his father. Since he was expecting his wife to take over the leadership of the marriage as his mother had done, she eventually obliged. The resulting problems finally sent them, in desperation, for help.

This is not to say that wives are to mindlessly stay in the background saying nothing but "Yes, dear." Real submission is not a passive thing. As Larry Christenson points out in *The Christian Family*, "Submission to authority means that you put yourself wholly at the disposal of the person who is set over you. This is the meaning that the Apostle Paul sets before the Christian in his submission to God: 'Yield yourselves to God . . . and your members to God as instruments of righteousness' (Romans 6:13). . . . If a wife withholds her understanding and feelings on a matter, she is being less than submissive, for she is not putting these things at her husband's disposal." In other words, submission is a positive thing, not a negative kind of giving in. It demands all of our intellectual, emotional, and spiritual resources. Unfortunately there are many Christian women who do not understand this. Because they have a very narrow understanding of what it is to submit, they simply watch and pray as their husbands go in the wrong direction and the family situation rapidly deteriorates around them. A wife who is truly supportive learns how to actively help her man to lead in the right direction. She sets the stage for discussions so that her husband can benefit from her insights.

One in Christ

Paul's words in Galatians 3:28 have been a problem for some people in trying to see what the Bible is saying about the role of women. The verse reads, "There is neither Jew nor Greek, there is neither slave nor free, there is neither male nor female; for you are all one in Christ Jesus." A cursory reading of that verse has led some to believe that Paul is saying that social, class, racial and sexual differences no longer exist or, at least, no longer have any meaning after we become Christians. As we study the entire passage more carefully, however, it becomes apparent that this is not the meaning of the text at all. It is obvious that Paul is not saying that as soon as a person becomes a Christian, he no longer is a member of a certain race, or a certain sex. No one would argue that. But neither is he saying that these differences no longer have meaning. It is also obvious that a slave who becomes a Christian is a slave still, with all the duties and hardships that go along with slavery. A Greek Christian is a Greek still, with any privileges that being a Greek may bring. In fact, Paul himself capitalized on his Roman citizenship. A wife who becomes a Christian remains in her position as wife with its responsibilities and privileges. Clearly Paul is speaking here of our position *in Christ*. He is talking about a vertical relationship (with God), not horizontal ones (with other Christians).

As the *Expositor's Greek Testament* puts it, "The Apostle finally repudiates every claim . . . on behalf of any distinct class to superior sanctity in Christ. All Christians, whatever their antecedents, are one in Christ." [1] No one may claim to be a better Christian, or more spiritual, simply because he belongs to a certain race, or, for that matter, a certain sex.

Herman Ridderbos in his commentary on Galatians has this to say, "The oneness of man and woman in Christ, illustrates how completely the bond in Christ conquers all things. . . . This is not to maintain that the natural and social distinction is in no respect relevant any more. From the point of view of redemption in Christ, however, and of the gifts of the Spirit granted by Him, there is no preference of Jew to Greek, master to slave, man to woman. This has social consequences, too, although the apostle does not enter further upon them at this point." [2] Certainly there are tremendous social implications in the gospel. But this text cannot be used to prove that everyone is "equal" in all social relationships.

Husbands Have Responsibility

So far we have been looking at what the Bible says about and to wives. Looking at the Ephesians passage again we see that it speaks as strongly to husbands as to wives. Their job is no less challenging. Verse 25 of chapter 5 reads, "Husbands, love your wives as Christ loves the church and gave himself up for her, that he might sanctify her . . ." Husbands must love their wives with a completely unselfish, in fact *self-sacrificing*, love. They are called to submerge their own egos for the sake of their wives' welfare. So they do not have the right to be "Lord of the castle" and give arbitrary orders to be obeyed. Their leadership is to be Christ-like. They must take responsibility for their wives' material and spiritual well-being. That's quite an order!

In *The Christian Family* Larry Christenson says that taking the spiritual leadership includes going the way of the Cross before one's wife. The husband must die to self. In practical matters this means, for example, being the first to humble himself and ask forgiveness in an argument with his wife even if "the wife's guilt is as great or greater. No matter. His call is to 'love his wife as Christ loved the church.' . . . As the spiritual head of the family, the husband and father must be the first to repent."

God holds men responsible for their wives' behavior. We see this already as we look at Adam and Eve in the Garden. Eve sinned first, yet Adam was held responsible. Eve wrongly made the decision *for the couple;* God nevertheless confronted Adam and held him accountable. He searched for Adam and asked for an explanation of what had happened. Adam then tried to evade the responsibility and push it off on his wife, as so many men have been trying to do ever since. So in the first sin of the first couple, we already see the two elements of an upside-down marriage. Adam did not give the proper spiritual leadership and then tried to abdicate responsibility; Eve, on the other hand, did not look to her husband for direction but took things into her own hands. Happily, God did not leave Adam and Eve at that point. He gave the promise which was redemptive. We also have the power of Christ and His word which can redeem us and our marriages.

Who Is to Handle the Finances?

One area in which a wife should be careful not to usurp her husband's authority is in the handling of the family's finances. Since the family's life-style is largely determined by how and where the family's money is spent, this is a vitally important matter. Family counsellors often say that money and sex are the subjects that cause the most marriage problems. Some even say that in the end almost all marriage problems can be reduced to money difficulties. Knowing how important it is that each partner have the proper relationship to Christ, I cannot agree with this.

A person who has a problem with his marriage partner has a problem with his relationship to God. Money, sex, in-laws—problems in these areas are manifestations of a deeper problem. However, the partners' attitude toward money and their handling of it are of major importance in a marriage. Money plays an important part in a family's life, in its health and well-being. Since this is so, it is necessary that the husband exercise his leadership in this area. Family finances are his responsibility, and the wife should not try to take this from him. He will, of course, delegate certain areas of financial responsibility to his wife. She will probably do most of the day-to-day purchasing of food, clothing, and household items. However, it is up to him to determine the family's financial priorities.

There are few things that emasculate a man so thoroughly as a wife who squanders the income he has worked so hard to provide. I remember a man sitting in our living room after his wife had left him. He told a sad story. One of the saddest parts was his discovery that he was many thousands of dollars in debt. His wife and he both worked full time and their combined income was quite impressive. He told us that he thought they were doing very well financially. But the pathetic thing was that he had no real knowledge of his financial situation. Each week he had simply handed his paycheck to his wife who in turn gave him some "pocket money." He had never cared to handle the money, he told us, so he had let his wife take care of it.

I also remember a young, successful lawyer talking to us about his money problems. He was nearly in tears as he told us that there was not even enough money to go away on a short vacation. Even though he was making three times as much as many of their friends, his wife managed to spend it all, often before they had it. He looked so bewildered as he told us that he never could really figure out where it all went. They did not have much to show for it. The money just seemed to slip through her fingers like sand.

Not all women are bad money managers, of course. Any study or survey would probably show that men and women do equally well (or badly) in this area. The point is that it is the husband's prerogative—his responsibility —to lead in financial matters. If his wife is taking the lead, whether she does a good job or a bad one, something has been subtracted from his manhood.

A Wife's Dreams Should Be Portable

Someone once said that a wife should make her dreams portable. She must be ready to follow her husband wherever the Lord leads him. Many a man's career has been thwarted, his potential nipped in the bud, because his wife would not leave the geographical area in which she preferred to live. It seems particularly tragic when this happens to pastors, but ministers' wives are not immune to this temptation. I know of one minister who decided that God was leading him to serve a church out West. He accepted the call, only to meet an ultimatum from his wife. She was simply not moving. It was either the church or her. The man regretfully reversed his decision. This was one situation that came out into the open. Most of them go on behind the scenes. But it is an open secret among pastors that certain men are hamstrung in a choice of location because of their wives.

It is not only pastors that God calls to relocate. There are many other men whose vocations demand that they move, often several times during their lives. Now I am not advocating more mobility for families. There are serious problems that accompany too-frequent moves. *No* relocation of an entire family is accomplished without a certain amount of tension and anxiety. I am not trying to minimize this. There are some men who become virtual nomads. They run from one job to another, from one part of the country to another, without regard to the devastating effects upon their families. These people are seeking happiness by changing their circumstances, which never works. In reality they are running away from themselves. But a man should be free to find God's will for his life without having to fit it into a framework set up for him by his wife. He should not have to say, "Lord, I'll go wherever you want, as long as it's not west of the Mississippi, because my wife won't live there."

Working at Marriage

It is worth mentioning here that it is not only the outspoken, aggressive wife who has trouble submitting to her husband. A quiet, clinging-vine type can sabotage her husband's leadership just as effectively. In fact, she can often be more destructive because she does not "fight fair." A man recognizes aggression in a woman and has a chance to deal with it. But the "weak" wife who cannot seem to cope hits below the belt. She appeals to her husband's protective nature. He certainly does not want to be a brute or a bully. He loves his wife and wants to take care of her. So when she pulls the poor-little-me—how-will-I-ever-manage routine, he gives in. She gets her way, and the husband often does not even realize that he is giving up his leadership. Weak people often manage to manipulate the strong.

In *Hidden Art* Edith Schaeffer says, "A good marriage does not just fall out of a tree, by itself." [3] Anyone who is successful in marriage will agree. It takes time and effort. And the greater part of that effort must come from the wife. That may not sound "fair," but that's the way it is. Working at marriage is one major part of homemaking. Our husbands are to give leadership, to provide for us and care for us materially and spiritually. They are required to spend a great deal of their time making a living for us and caring for us in other ways. We, also, must spend a great deal of time and effort caring for our husbands' needs. We do this when we cook or iron shirts. But a wife must also spend time and thought caring for her husband's emotional needs. This is what I mean by "working at marriage." A wife must study her husband to find out what his individual needs are. And this study will continue for a lifetime. As a man grows and changes, his needs may change.

Every husband needs a wife who is loving and devoted. Every man also needs his home to have a basic degree of cleanliness and neatness. There are some Christians whose homes are indescribably messy and dirty. I have never been one to advocate paying excessive attention to housekeeping chores. Compulsive housekeepers, like other victims of compulsive behavior, have a problem. But there is a vast difference between a somewhat casual approach to housekeeping and the virtual neglect that one sees in some homes. One woman of my acquaintance has been praying for some time for her husband to become a Christian. But her house is in such terrible shape that one actually becomes nauseated from the stench. There are piles of dirty dishes and garbage, the diaper pail is overflowing, and everything is in confusion. This woman has much to learn about the art of being a wife before she can expect her prayers for her husband to be answered. Right now she is standing in the way of his seeing Christ.

Another thing that is important to all husbands is the appearance of their wives. Women who let themselves become excessively heavy, or neglect to pay proper attention to their hair or clothes are not meeting their husbands' needs. A friend of mine who recently lost a great deal of weight said that it has done wonders for her marriage. She had not realized how much her being fat had bothered her husband until she dieted. Of course a woman can err in the other direction as well. We must not spend over-much money or time on our hairdos and clothes. In fact, this extreme is probably a temptation to more women than the other. But being a Christian is no reason to be dowdy.

All husbands desire their wives to be loving, attractive, and decent housekeepers. But when it comes to specifics, each man has different emotional needs to be met. One man may crave a house that is always in perfect order—messiness offends him to the very core of his being. If you have a man like this, it is your responsibility to make every effort to have the house in shape when he returns in the evening. (I am thankful that my husband is not one of these. A modest amount of disarray does nothing to dampen his spirits.)

At a conference my husband and I attended recently, one of the speakers was a prominent Christian psychologist. His wife led one session for the wives in which she related an incident from her own life that was helpful to us. When she and her husband were first married she never made the bed until late in the day. She would turn the covers back and open the windows so the bed could "air out." This frustrated her husband whose sense of the rightness of things included a bed that was immediately made up. Finally she realized that she was letting this relatively minor detail get in the way of her relationship with her husband. She has been making the bed before breakfast ever since. This taught me some things in my own life. You can build a stronger relationship by getting many of the details out of the way.

In a lot of these little things it really does not matter who is "right." One man needs a wife who is outgoing, who is well-read and can intelligently discuss a number of topics with him. My husband is a news-hound. Political science has always fascinated him. Consequently, I am always thoroughly versed on the current world crisis, whatever it may be, although my personal inclination is to let the Arabs and Israelis worry about their own problems. It is a wife's responsibility to have her antennae out so that she can discover her husband's needs and meet them.

In an article from the Nov. '71 *Family Circle* entitled "How to Make a Good Marriage Great," Abigail (Dear Abby) Van Buren says, "How does a woman make a good marriage great? That's easy. She simply works like a dog at it. . . . If you're beginning to think (making marriage work) is mostly up to the woman, then you're getting the message. Women's Libbers may stone me, but I've always felt that way. In fact, it's the only 'fact of life' my mother ever told me."

It is just as difficult for many men to give proper leadership as it is for many women to follow. Leadership is never easy. There are risks to be taken, new paths to be charted. It demands courage, discipline, and strength of character. It is often much easier to let the wife take over, particularly if she is a strong-willed person. I constantly thank the Lord that He gave me a husband who is capable of leading me.

However, it is not ultimately in our husbands that we find fulfillment. True fulfillment is found only in being grounded in Christ and doing His will. As the Bible points out, His will for wives is following their husbands' leadership.

CHAPTER 2

Keeping the Proper Perspective

For most women, becoming a wife includes running a home. This involves housework—the countless big and little chores and tasks that go into the smooth operation of a home. This aspect of homemaking has gotten badly out of focus in recent years.

On the one hand there are those who take a very negative view of housework. To them it is nothing but mopping, ironing, washing dishes, and cooking. Day after day the same monotonous chores. Some, particularly those with small children, feel themselves caught in a treadmill. They keep plugging away at an endless round of menial tasks. They are never finished, yet they never seem really to accomplish anything. Housework for them is incredibly boring and stifling to the imagination. Women's magazines are full of stories about "trapped housewives" and their problems.

Others, realizing the importance of housework, go to another extreme. They are the spotless housekeepers who, in Peg Bracken's words, "won't stop." They give top priority to a house which is gleaming from top to bottom at all times. "Cleanliness is next to godliness" is their motto. (They are sure it is in the Bible somewhere.) And woe be to a child who leaves an apple core in the living room! In some circles the highest praise that can be spoken about a woman is, "You can eat from her floors."

Now if we think about this for a minute, we realize that occasions for eating from floors are very few and far between. Jesus had something to say to a woman who got carried away with her chores. Martha was "distracted by her many tasks" when Jesus was visiting in her home. She was frustrated because her sister Mary, instead of helping her, was calmly sitting listening to Jesus. Martha thought Jesus should reprimand her and tell her to "lend a hand." To her surprise, Jesus told Martha that her priorities were all wrong. "Martha, Martha, you are fretting and fussing about so many things; but one thing is necessary. The part that Mary has chosen is best; and it shall not be taken away from her" (Luke 10:40-42, NEB).

There are still others, as we saw in the first chapter, who seem to do no housework at all. Either they scorn these tasks as beneath them, or they are so lazy and undisciplined that they just never get around to them. These women cannot really be called homemakers at all. They are simply living in their houses; they are not making them into homes.

How can we get housework into the proper perspective? How can we try to find God's will for us in this seemingly mundane part of our lives? The answer to these questions has two parts.

First, we must realize that housework is necessary, and there is nothing demeaning about it. It is important from God's point of view. You may wince at the corny little poems seen in some kitchens about serving the Lord while washing pots and pans, but the idea is right on target. The Lord has called many of us to wash pots and pans, to say nothing about piles of diapers. We must do these things "as unto the Lord." And let us not be fooled by all the propaganda abroad today into thinking that homemaking has more than its share of drudgery. All jobs include "chores," no matter how glamorous they may sound, and homemaking has more than its share of creative aspects. In our increasingly complex, depersonalizing and dehumanizing society, it is more important than ever that our homes be havens for our husbands and children. The woman who creates a pleasant atmosphere for the family members to revive their spirits for facing another day's work and service is making a real contribution.

Second, we must not lose sight of the fact that housework is only a part of homemaking. Once our daily chores are finished there are many other things waiting for our attention. Proper nurture of our children takes time. There are people who need to be told of Jesus' love, people who need our "cup of cold water." There are lonely, discouraged people in need of our help—some desperately in need. There are worthy "causes" to be championed. There is a whole world to be redeemed. Christian homes can be centers in the larger community, integral parts of a large network of concern helping to hold together the fabric of society.

To accomplish this, our aim should be to do the least pleasant, most routine chores as quickly and efficiently as possible in order to get on with the more creative parts of housework. Then when our housework is finished, we can move on to other areas of service. The amount of time that a woman spends on housework and how she spends the rest of her time is largely an individual matter. She will decide this prayerfully, taking into consideration her family's needs and her own talents. A woman with small children will have considerably less time to reach out than a woman whose children are older or have left home.

Keeping a Schedule Will Help

How can we learn to do our chores quickly and well? One big part of the answer is quite obvious, but it escaped me for quite some time. It is simply this—a homemaker must have a schedule.

I came to homemaking under somewhat unusual circumstances. With stars in my eyes I crammed my last year of college into one semester so I could sail off to be married in Europe where my fiancé was studying. We had a six-week honeymoon, traveling all over the Continent in our vintage Citroen. Then we settled down in Amsterdam for a couple of years with a few months' stay in Switzerland thrown in. It was all very exciting. There were so many things to do—museums and shops to explore, languages to learn, and then markets where I could try my proficiency in Dutch, German or French. (My German consists of a handful of words superimposed onto Dutch, but it often worked.) Housework tended to take a back seat. It was not that I scorned it. I rather enjoyed it, particularly the cooking part. I tried new recipes at quite a clip and even invented a few of my own. But since living in Europe is a once-in-a-lifetime experience for most Americans, I was determined to make the most of it. So our living tended to be quite casual.

Also, much of what I knew about homemaking did not apply in my situation. I had none of the labor-saving devices that Americans consider necessities, such as a refrigerator, a vacuum cleaner, or a washing machine, to say nothing of a dryer. (I think that given a choice between a washer and dryer, I would have chosen the latter, since some articles of clothing took several days to dry in Amsterdam's damp climate.) The marketing had to be done daily, going from one specialty store to the other. I made my daily round of the baker, the butcher, the green-grocer, and the cheese merchant.

So when we returned to the United States my situation was quite different. Soon I had my second baby, twenty-one months after the first. By this time we were in a large parsonage, and I was swamped. I was doing a lot of entertaining. including many overnight guests, plus being quite involved in church work. Somewhere along the line I realized that if order was to prevail in our household, I was going to have to impose it. I was reacting a bit against any kind of schedule because I had had experiences with people whose schedules ran their lives— people who could not come to an important church meeting because "we always grocery shop on Thursday evenings." Their schedules were like the law of the Medes and Persians. They were willing to show mercy if it could be worked in, say, between one and two o'clock on Friday afternoon.

Besides, I was working hard from the time I got up until after the dinner dishes were finished, and often until bedtime. What difference could arranging or rearranging my chores make? They all had to be done, I reasoned. Finally it somehow got through to me that a schedule *does* make a difference. It must be kept flexible, to be sure. On some days the whole thing has to be ignored— a child is suddenly very sick, or unexpected company drops in. But there is one thing you will discover: you get very few interruptions before nine or ten o'clock in the morning. So if you "stick with it" and get your basic chores over by then, you will be much more serene about meeting the rest of the day, whatever it includes.

A woman's schedule must be tailored to her individual needs and the needs of her family. Also, it changes as circumstances change. A new baby obviously means drastic alterations in the schedule. The youngest child's entrance into school will also change things. I find that at least once a year I must re-work my schedule. At present it looks like the one on the following page.

Two afternoons a week I lead a prayer group for an hour and a half. Others I spend making calls, sewing, or practicing the piano. You may wonder about the ab-

	7:30-8:00	8:00-8:30	8:30-9:00	9:00-9:30	9:30-11:30	11:30-11:45
Mon.	Breakfast and family devotions	Dress, fix lunches (girls do beds and dishes)	Do a load of wash, handwash, or whatever quick dusting and sweeping needs to be done	Devotions	A special cleaning project (cleaning the refrigerator, oven, closets, etc.) or making calls depending on need	Iron the 2 or 3 items from the day's wash
Tues.	``	``	``	``	``	``
Wed.	``	``	``	``	``	``
Thurs.	``	``	``	``	Grocery shop, run errands (dry cleaners, shoe repair, etc.)	``
Fri.	``	``	``	``	Dust and vacuum main floor	``
Sat.	``	``	``	``	Practice the piano (girls clean the bathrooms and their own rooms)	

sence of certain chores on my list—doing the dishes, for instance. I have the great blessing of having four daughters, apprentice homemakers all, so I no longer do dishes, or sort and put away wash, or several other chores. In fact, while I was writing this book the older ones took over the preparation of four dinners a week, plus most of the ironing, vacuuming, and baking. The younger ones helped as much as they were able.

Your schedule may look quite different. The point is, when I did not have my time organized, my chores ran me; now I can master them. I thought a schedule would be arbitrary and restrictive, but it turned out to be quite the opposite. It can give freedom. God is a God of order, and He seems to use us and our talents best in an orderly fashion.

Some Things "Don't Need Doing"

Another thing to keep in mind while doing housekeeping chores is that, as Peg Bracken says in *The I Hate to Housekeep Book*, "Many things—regardless of what the experts say—don't need doing." [4] And there are also "things you needn't do half so often as the experts would have you believe." For instance, every bed does not necessarily have to be changed every week. A lot depends on the color of the sheets, the size of the bed, and the person sleeping in it. Change the sheets when they need changing. During our brief residence in Switzerland, we discovered that the Swiss changed their sheets every six weeks. Learning this helped me to get the subject in perspective. Windows are something else that many women are led to believe need constant attention. Except for the ones your toddler fingerprints, they can go nicely for weeks and weeks between cleanings. Of course the house must be basically clean. But beware of being cowed into doing unnecessary housework. Take a fresh look at your chores and set your own standards, taking your family's needs and your talents and responsibilities in other areas into consideration.

Teamwork

Before we go any further, there is one point that should be clarified. The Bible clearly speaks of a leadership role for the husband and a submissive role for the wife. However, I do not think this means that there can be no flexibility in deciding who does which chores around the house. If a couple has no children and the wife has an outside job, it would be unfair of the husband to expect her to carry the full responsibility for the housework as well. Even full-time homemakers can often expect their husbands to help with some of the chores, depending on the circumstances. Each individual couple will work these details out for themselves.

A man's role as leader is not endangered nor his masculinity threatened by the performance of any given task. My husband, for example, has been making the breakfast for the family for several years. I only make it on Mondays (his day off) and when we have guests. In the first years of our marriage we considered it to be a part of my job. Then as the babies came and I was up during the night to nurse them, he started making breakfast for me. Now we have settled into this routine, which suits us both. I, on the other hand, often run errands and help him with chores which have to do with his work. The purpose of this book is not to quibble about such things. My aim is to look at the tremendous range of possibilities in homemaking: to show that it is a career as varied, challenging, and stimulating as any open to man or woman.

CHAPTER 3

Creative Housekeeping

The whole area of food planning and preparation is an important part of homemaking. A woman can do a lot to express her creativity while planning menus and cooking for her family and friends. Living in this technical age is a distinct advantage for us. We have a vast array of convenience foods, some of them more delicious than anything Grandmother made, in spite of the nostalgia which surrounds her cooking. On the other hand, there are some prepared mixes that are pretty bad imitations of the real thing, and take almost as much time into the bargain. If we want to prepare all our food completely "from scratch," we are quite free to do so. The results will probably be better than at any time in history, since our ingredients tend to be fresher and more varied, and our equipment is usually excellent.

A woman who regards herself as a professional homemaker will use prepared mixes and other convenience foods, but she will not rely on them too much. This is partly because all that convenience costs money, sometimes a great deal. Also it is very satisfying, for instance, to put together something like a big batch of soup and smell it simmering on the back of the stove all day. If you are not in the habit of making soup, let me suggest that you begin. You can improvise to your heart's content; there are almost limitless possibilities. Besides satisfying the palate (and the spirit as well), it is a marvelous way to be economical.

Every time I have liquid left from cooked vegetables I pour it into a jar in the refrigerator. I also save all gravy— beef, chicken, pork—the more the better. I keep any dabs of peas, beans, corn, rice, etc., in a plastic container in the freezer. When it is time to make soup again, in they all go, along with the remains of catsup which gets rinsed out of the bottle. I have put my basic recipe in the back of the book. I make this soup quite thick, its only accompaniment my mother's graham gems* (muffins). This graham gem recipe has been in our family for generations. It originally included "shortening the size of two eggs"; an enterprising aunt made the translation to "a stick of margarine." The muffins are stirred up in fifteen minutes and bake in another fifteen.

Have you tried baking bread? Here is something that can involve your family. Let me warn you that unless no one is around when you take it out of the oven, the first loaf will disappear before it has time to cool! Our twelve-year-old enjoys the bread-making ritual so much that she has all but taken it over from me. The others all love to help when it is time for punching the dough. You can make dinner rolls, cinnamon buns, and several other things from one basic recipe. There is something very satisfying about working with dough. It is interesting to see that many young people are beginning to bake their own bread. For many of them the whole process is full of symbolism—of going back to the earth, of hospitality. I personally think

---

* Recipe in back of book.

that no child should have to grow up without ever tasting homemade bread fresh from the oven with the butter melting on it!

Do experiment when you cook. I happen to like inventing my own recipes, and sometimes I get a little help. One of my favorite recipes for pie, rhubarb-raisin, was my husband's idea. When I was making my first rhubarb pie as a new bride he asked, "Aren't you going to put raisins in it? My mother always puts raisins in her rhubarb pies." The idea sounded all right to me, so I reduced the sugar a bit and added a double fistful of raisins. The result was very good—the dried raisins absorbed some of the excess liquid from the rhubarb and the taste was tantalizingly tart-sweet. The dessert became one of our favorites. Some time later while visiting my husband's parents I offered to make a rhubarb pie. Watching me, my mother-in-law said, "Oh, do you put raisins in it?" My husband still has not figured out where his idea came from!

It is not necessary to devise your own recipes. Cookbooks and magazines are bursting with recipes waiting to be tried. If you have gotten into a rut with the same old menus week after week, you could set aside a day a week for trying a new recipe. One time it might be a main dish, the next time a dessert.

Your cooking and baking can provide you with presents that you know will always be welcome. There is no worry about the proper size or color, and you are able to give a little of yourself with your gift. When I make jam I always set aside a few jars for this purpose. You can be sure homemade cookies will be accepted with pleasure. My fruitcake* has become one of our Christmas traditions. The children all help in this project, cutting up fruit or mixing the batter. Every year I mail out about a dozen cakes. They have gone as far as Vietnam and Nigeria.

The recipe came about while we were living in Cali-

---

* Recipe in back of book.

fornia. We had seven apricot trees which produced prolifically. We dried several hundred pounds of these cots every year, so I was always looking for new uses for them. After much experimenting in search of the "right" fruitcake, I settled on a rich combination of fruits and nuts, including many apricots, in a light batter. My friends and family tell me they look forward to receiving the cakes every year.

Nutrition is more important today than ever before, and this aspect of her family's health is the homemaker's responsibility. Only a generation ago it was fairly simple to meet a family's nutritional needs. The basic foods—meat, dairy products, fruits, vegetables, and grain products—were easily available and usually quite simply prepared. Our mothers and grandmothers did not have nearly the variety of fruits and vegetables available the year round that we do, but they stored the ones they could for the winter. They used some refined and processed foods, but the amount and variety of these were limited as well. A more thorough knowledge of nutrition was not necessary, since by just eating what was available most families fared pretty well. But in the last few decades there has been a fantastic proliferation of food products: natural foods, semi-processed foods, fully processed foods, and what might be called non-foods. Diet soda pop is an example of an item in this last category. It is nothing but a collection of chemicals, hopefully not too harmful, with no nutritive value whatsoever.

A homemaker can no longer take what is available from her grocer and assume that her family's needs will be met. There is simply too much available which is of questionable value. She must become informed on the subject of nutrition so that she can guard her family's health and well-being. Women's magazines often contain excellent articles on nutrition. A good source of free booklets and pamphlets on the subject is your county extension office. The people in these offices are there to serve you; they are glad to help. Drop in if it is not too far away, or write to them. There are also many good books on the subject, some available in paperback.

Providing a Pleasant Physical Atmosphere

By creating a pleasant physical atmosphere in the home, we can bring out some of our best talents, and at the same time make a worthwhile contribution to our family and friends. It is a very satisfying form of self-expression and can contribute to our own sense of well-being. We often take our surroundings for granted, yet they have a great effect on us. Of course it must be made clear that all material possessions must be viewed in the proper light. Ostentation is never godly. Keeping up with the Joneses with their homes and furnishings is probably a big temptation to some Christians. This is a sin, and we should see it as such. But God is a God of beauty as well as order, and He has given us beautiful things to enjoy.

One manisfestation of His image in us is our ability to create. Our creativity is limited and flawed, but nonetheless real. One way we can develop this ability is by using color, fabric, paint, and whatever else is necessary to create aesthetic surroundings: rooms which are pleasant, cheerful, and even beautiful. Some of us have more talent than others in this respect. I have a friend with taste in decorating so unerring that it is akin to the gift of perfect pitch some musicians possess. Not many of us are so fortunate. But with practice our talents for decorating can blossom.

Money is not of prime importance here. There is no price tag on taste. It is nice to be able to afford wall-to-wall carpeting or an expensive sofa, but not at all essential. I have been in spacious homes where the furniture was expensive and every square foot was carpeted, yet the total effect was empty. There was no elegance, charm or grace, nothing to reflect the individuality and personality of whoever lived there. I have also been in homes where warmth and elegance were achieved with refurbished secondhand furniture and imaginative accessories.

Color is a marvelous decorating tool. Make use of bright, bold colors. Black, white, and scarlet can make a dramatic room. (Someday, somewhere, I hope to have a bright red carpet!) Vivid yellows and oranges with brown can be lovely. My own house is full of clear, bright shades of blue, along with touches of purple and green. Be sure to use large blocks of color. You will not achieve the hoped-for effect with small bits of color here and there. "Thinking big" is a good rule to follow in accessorizing any room, unless it is very tiny. Small accents scattered about only create a cluttered effect. If you want to use small items, mass them. Group several items on a wall—paintings, collages, mirrors. Use several containers of flowers together.

Paintings and other wall decorations need not be expensive. If you have talent in this direction, by all means paint your own pictures. They may never be collector's items, but if they have color and grace they will be enjoyed. And you will have originals! I much prefer originals of this type to the often mediocre reproductions of the same few pictures one encounters so often. Neither my husband nor I have a smidgen of ability to draw or paint, but we have some paintings that friends have done for us, and they give us a great deal of pleasure.

Although you cannot paint, you could probably make a collage. If your first effort is not suitable for display, try again. You can use fabric scraps: bright pieces of velvet or linen make a lovely effect. Abstractions using geometric shapes are easiest to do. Or you can use different kinds of grasses, weeds, seeds, and pine cones. I recently saw a stunning collage which was nothing more than a very large sheet of cork completely covered with small pieces of driftwood fitted next to each other.

It was a beautiful example of understated elegance. Whatever you choose to do in the area of decorating, remember that your house is sending a message to all who enter. Be sure it is the message you want sent.

Flower Arranging

In Japan flower arranging, called *Ikebana*, is considered one of the important arts. Men, women, and children study its principles, and it has had a profound effect on their people. In the Netherlands flowers are considered to be a common, everyday necessity, like bread or cheese. They are raised as a regular crop and sold on every street corner. Since my husband and I were married in the Netherlands, as a young bride I learned to make flowers a part of my life. Even a tiny apartment with ungainly furniture and impossible wallpaper can be brightened by the addition of a bowl of daffodils. Flowers in Holland enhance all occasions, small or great. No self-respecting guest would show up for dinner or a party without a bunch of tulips or hyacinths to hand his hostess.

Except for some areas of California (notably San Francisco), one cannot usually buy flowers that easily or cheaply here. But in the summer most of us can grow our own, and in the fall we can probably manage to get near some countryside to collect dried wild flowers and weeds which can be used in arrangements. Perhaps a place could even be found in the budget to buy a carnation or three from the florist in the dead of winter! We in the Northwest are fortunate in this respect. Flowers bloom here about eight months of the year, and when all the flowers have given up we can usually find some berries and evergreens to arrange.

Here are some of the basic principles of flower arranging. First, keep a variety of vases and containers handy. I find a bud vase indispensable for those times when I discover a single rose on one of our bushes. Almost anything can serve as a container. For shallow containers, such as a fruitbowl, you will need a "frog" in which to anchor the stems. (Some of the most successful arrangements are made with a frog because you have more control over the direction of the flowers and greenery.) Several things in your china closet will work, including your tea set. Try arranging similar bouquets in a coffeepot, teapot, and sugarbowl to grace your dining room table.

Second, except for a mass of small flowers, use an uneven number of blooms. If you are combining large and small flowers, use an uneven number of the large ones. Also, it is usually best to use the bigger blooms near the base of the arrangement, to avoid a top-heavy look. The same is true for the most vivid colors. In a bouquet of red, pink, and white flowers, for example, the red ones would be closest to the center. Another thing to remember is to keep the size of the arrangement in proper proportion to the container. When you are using a low, shallow container the height of your arrangement should be about one and a half to two times the width of the container.

These suggestions are only meant to be helpful. Do not let them get in the way. Take your flowers and a bowl, follow your own creative instincts, and then enjoy the results!

I cannot leave this subject without a word about artificial flowers. Nothing is more characteristic of the plastic age we live in—carefully contrived "beauty," invulnerable and sterile. There is too much artificiality around us everywhere, both in relationships and in things. Many man-made fibers and materials have proven to be of superior durability and have become indispensable. We are glad that synthetics make a variety of things available to us that would otherwise be either beyond our reach or impractical. But for sheer beauty, leather, wool, and silk win every time. And no imitation can even come close to matching the beauty of real flowers. If fresh flowers are not available to you for the picking and you cannot afford to buy them, use dried field flowers and weeds. These can be sprayed different colors if you wish. Just use an aerosol can of spray paint. Or you can buy bunches of straw flowers which are professionally dried. Pussywillows if cut in full "bloom" and left out of water will last indefinitely. All of these have natural beauty which can communicate itself to us. Plastic flowers can do nothing to nourish the spirit.

Sewing Has Its Place

Sewing is one aspect of homemaking which is regaining importance. Some twenty or thirty years ago home sewing was usually done for the sole purpose of saving money. Children often despaired of their homemade outfits and envied the store-bought clothes their friends wore. Sometimes a special event such as graduation would be the occasion for a shopping trip to town to buy a ready-made frock. Now all that is changed.

My oldest daughter recently told me that she is a little embarrassed when she is complimented on a new outfit and has to admit that neither she herself nor I made it. To admit to having simply gone shopping for clothes evidently shows a lack of imagination or skill. I must confess to similar feelings. There is a tremendous satisfaction in successfully sewing an outfit. You can be as original as you please, and save tidy sums of money into the bargain. It is also possible to go on to design your own clothes after you have mastered the basic sewing skills and have learned to work with patterns. The young seem to be in the vanguard of the new trend. A recent survey showed that 87 percent of teen-aged girls now make at least some of their clothes. Whether it is to save money or to express their individuality was not indicated. Perhaps it is a combination of both.

Sewing, like cooking, can provide you with welcome

gifts for special occasions or just to say "I love you." Some of us in our congregation have started making ties for our husbands and friends. They are simple and quick to make, cost a fraction of the price of ready-mades, and our men are delighted. My husband, who has never paid more than casual attention to his clothes, preferring to ignore the whole subject and let me pick them out, is now inordinately proud of his extensive tie collection. He all but refuses to wear any that I have not sewn.

Along with increased interest in sewing and other do-it-yourself projects, patchwork is being revived. Perhaps the necessity for ecological concern also has something to do with it. This is certainly recycling at its best. Attractive clothes can be made, at virtually no cost, from materials that would otherwise be discarded. Making a patchwork skirt or dress from your own fabric scraps is a sure way of having a one-of-a-kind garment. It can also evoke many pleasant memories. I have a skirt and matching vest made of patches from scraps collected over the years. Wearing it is a little like wearing a charm bracelet: This patch is from my pantsuit, this velvet is from the dress I had before Kathy was born, these are from Dad's ties. It even contains some of the fabric from my wedding dress.

There are some things that I have learned in working with patchwork that I think are worth passing on. First, pick one or two basic colors that will appear in all your patches. My vest and skirt are all shades of blue and purple. Many other colors are included, but each square contains at least some blue or purple and these are the only solid colors that are used. In other garments I have used gold and red, or shades of beige and brown.

Another thing to remember is to use patches that are similar in weight. If you try sewing a very light-weight cotton, for instance, to a heavy velveteen or corduroy, it may pucker. With this in mind, you can use almost any fabric for patchwork. Wools are beautiful, as are napped fabrics such as different types of corduroy, plush, and velvet. I have used velveteens and corduroys in combination with linens and heavy-weight cottons. The more lush fabric squares are an elegant addition to the everyday cottons. Also, be sure that you pick a simple design with a minimum of seams and no trimming. For skirts I use a basic A-line pattern with a side zipper so that there are only two main pattern pieces. Using your pattern as a guide, put together only as much "fabric" as you need. I use five-inch squares. They can be larger or smaller, but I find this size to be the most attractive and easiest to handle. I sew the squares in horizontal rows and then put the rows together. But before I sew a stitch I lay out the entire garment to be sure the design is what I want. Remember to color-coordinate your garment at the seams the way you would match a plaid. This designing the color pattern is the most fun: arranging large and small prints and solids together to form a harmonious whole.

There are many other possibilities for creative housekeeping. This chapter is in no way meant to be the last word on the subject. Nor does it mean to imply that every homemaker must master all of these skills. It is merely intended to show something of the scope of our profession, even before we begin to branch out beyond our "housework."

CHAPTER 4

Hospitality and Counseling

Hebrews 13:2 talks about "entertaining angels un-
awares." On one occasion when my husband and I fol-
lowed the admonition of this verse, the stranger in our
home turned out to be a considerably less-than-angelic
character. He had come to our door with a tale of woe.
My husband was not entirely convinced by his story,
but we invited him to stay to dinner and packed him
a lunch to take on his way. A few days later we saw
his picture in the paper, along with a report stating that
he was wanted by the FBI on several different charges,
including armed robbery of a bank.

At other times we have entertained persons who we
knew were lawbreakers. I think of Joe, who had shot
his wife, intending to kill her before aiming the gun
at his own head. He fainted before he could do so,
and by the time he revived the police were there. His
wife did not die, but remained badly disfigured. While he
was out on bail awaiting trial, even his best friends were
too afraid to see him. My husband and I invited him

into our home where we were able to minister to him, and he became a Christian. While he served his time in prison, he was a real witness for Christ. When we saw the trusted position he was given in prison, we were reminded of the story of Joseph. The warden depended on him for so much that he said he would be sorry to see him leave when he had served his time.

These are unusual cases. Not many of us are called on to entertain bank robbers or murderers. But hospitality is an important Christian virtue. It was required of the Old Testament Israelites. Deuteronomy 10:18 and 20 says: "The Lord your God . . . loves the alien who lives among you, giving him food and clothing. You too must love the alien, for you once lived as aliens in Egypt." This is a recurring theme in the Old Testament. "Remember, you too were strangers." The command to show kindness to strangers was linked to the Israelites' deliverance from Egypt. It was to be a response to God's kindness to them. The deliverance from the slavery of Egypt is a picture of our deliverance from the slavery of sin. So our response as New Testament people of God and recipients of His grace should certainly be no less.

Hospitality is stated as a qualification for elders in I Timothy 3:2. In Romans 12:13 Paul speaks to all of us when he says, "Get into the habit of inviting guests home for dinner or, if they need lodging, for the night" (Living Bible). Of course, circumstances are different today. We have motels and restaurants readily available and most travelers can well afford to pay for them. I am not suggesting that it is necessary or even desirable for us to accommodate vacationers, for instance. This is not what the Bible is talking about. Nor does most of our entertaining of friends and relatives qualify as hospitality in the Biblical sense. There is no particular virtue in having someone to dinner who will return the favor in a few weeks. This may be a fine practice, but it does not come under the heading of Biblical hospitality. The

Bible talks about ministering *to those in need.* Jesus makes this very explicit in Luke 14:12-14 when He says, "When you put on a dinner . . . don't invite friends, brothers, relatives, and rich neighbors! For they will return the invitation. Instead, invite the poor, the crippled, the lame and the blind. Then at the resurrection of the godly, God will reward you for inviting those who can't repay you" (Living Bible).

Opportunities Unlimited

Keeping this in mind we see that there is a real ministry in hospitality for the homemaker. There are people all around us with physical, emotional, or spiritual needs to be met. Even as the poor are "always with us," so there are still people who need a meal or a bed that we can give them. When my husband and I were in our first parsonage, on the prairie, an occasional tramp would come asking for a handout. Since I was alone in the house except for my babies, I would not invite him in. I would give him a cup of coffee and a sandwich to eat on our back step. It was always very satisfying to be able to feed someone who was really in need. No vagabonds ever come to our present home, but perhaps this is not very common anymore. We recently did have the opportunity to show hospitality to a young man with physical needs as well as emotional problems. He was not quite to the point of being able to work, although the mental hospital had dismissed him as healthy. While he was in a rehabilitation program, he stayed with us since he was financially unable to provide for himself.

Sometimes an opportunity does arise to take in a stranger in the Old Testament sense. A few years ago a young girl appeared at the doorsteps of our church, suitcase and personal belongings in hand. She had just become a Christian in a town some distance away. The person that led her to Christ told her she should come to our church; so she quit her job, packed up, and came. One of the elders had an extra room in his house, and he and his wife agreed to take her in. This woman befriended her and helped to make her feel part of the church. The girl's background was quite different from that of most of the church members, and at times there was a distinct lack of communication between them. But the women of the church were able to get through to her by demonstrating that they were truly concerned about her. She is now married to a fine Christian and has become a member of the church. I will never forget the night we gave her a surprise shower. I almost decided we should not have made it a surprise. It looked as if she might collapse on the spot. She was so touched that we cared that much. She kept saying over and over, "I didn't know I had so many friends." I am quite sure that she now knows she "belongs," and it happened because Christ's people were able to show His love to her.

Ministering to the Single and Lonely

There are many other people who are not physically in need of our hospitality, yet their needs are as real. There are many lonely people with whom we come in contact, who very much need to be invited to our homes. Sometimes we who are so busy all day, every day, and are surrounded by people all the time, have a hard time realizing that other people are lonely.

There are many single people who seldom have the opportunity to enjoy a meal with a family. You could start by inviting the single people in your church and your neighborhood. It will be a treat for them on two counts: because of the family atmosphere, and because they often do not prepare substantial meals for themselves. Think a minute: if you lived alone, how often would you make a pot roast, potatoes and gravy, a salad, vegetable, and dessert? This is quite an ordinary meal for most families, but something special for a person who lives alone. Even two single people who live together do not always cook well-balanced meals. Perhaps even more important than the food is the knowledge that you care enough about them to invite them over.

On any college campus there are always a few students who are unable to go home for the various holidays. Some of them live too far away, others do not have the money to travel. It is a desolate feeling for a young person to be one of a handful of people eating a holiday dinner in a dormitory cafeteria. If there is a college in your town, you could include one or two of them in your festivities. You might even be able to host a foreign student. This would be a rewarding experience for your whole family as well as for the student.

College students are not the only ones who may be lonely on a holiday. Perhaps a young family has recently moved into your neighborhood. They have no relatives nearby with whom they can celebrate. You can be their "family" for the occasion. On the other hand, perhaps *you* have just moved into a new community and are feeling blue when you think about Thanksgiving or Christmas with only your little family. You can take the initiative and invite someone to your home. It is hard to have the blues while you are busy making someone else happy. If you are not yet well enough acquainted with your neighbors to know whom to invite, call your pastor. He will know which people in the church or community could be ministered to in this way.

The happiest and most fulfilled homemakers are those who are consistently ministering to others in addition to their own families. *Kaffee-klatches* have become an object of scorn to many people who see them as a symbol of all that is inane and superficial in the life of the modern housewife. It is true that some women do sit together over endless cups of coffee, exchanging trivia. But a great deal of concern, wisdom, and love can be dispensed along with a cup of coffee. Important matters can be discussed over coffee in a woman's kitchen just as well as in a college student union, a coffee house, or a pastor's study.

In Action as God's Co-workers

In an article entitled "Counseling" in the January 30, 1970 *Banner*, Rolf Veenstra reports on an interesting experiment carried out by the staff of a Christian psychiatric hospital. "A group of average housewives was given some rudimentary instruction in the basics of counseling and 'turned loose' on some genuine, typical psychological cases. In many ways their results were as good as the professionals'. This says something as to the growing need for counseling within the church. The temptation is to load the pastor with it ... (but) it is something that *every* member of Christ's body should share." [5] I am quite sure that the author did not intend to imply that we homemakers are qualified to deal with all the problems that we meet in the people who cross our paths. Some must certainly be given over to professional counselors. But a great many of the problems people experience today are spiritual at the core. So a homemaker who has the security of being firmly Christ-directed can be of tremendous help in counseling people. I have seen this happen time after time.

In *Competent to Counsel* Jay E. Adams says, "Man is born in sin ... and will ... attempt various sinful dodges in an attempt to avoid facing up to his sin. ... Apart from organically generated difficulties, the 'mentally ill' are really *people with unsolved personal problems.*" [6] He contends that such people are not carrying a load of false guilt around. They really *are* guilty, and must confess their sin in order to be helped. Christians who possess the qualities of goodness and knowledge and, most importantly, are "conversant with the Scriptures" can help troubled people where non-Christian psychiatrists cannot. The reason that non-Christians are not competent to counsel is that "counseling is the work

56

of the Holy Spirit." [7] Adams goes on to say that although the pastor is exceptionally qualified as a counselor because of his Biblical training, "all Christians, not simply ministers of the Gospel, should engage in it." [8]

I remember one case where a young wife and mother with a history of mental illness had been almost incoherent for several days. The husband was asking that she be hospitalized again. Then one of her acquaintances who has a vital relationship with Christ went to visit her. The change was astounding. She immediately was able to carry on a normal conversation with the woman. This woman related to me that her young friend seemed to be reaching out for the strength that she had. The young mother was severely troubled by guilt. When this woman talked to her about God's remedy for our guilt (which she had never heard of before!), reading some of the pertinent Bible passages, she began to respond. Her doctor also saw an improvement in her as she continued visiting with this woman and reading the Bible.

Contacts That Count

I also think of a dear friend and relative whose home is, by her own definition, a bit like Grand Central Station. She has five children of her own and a foster daughter, but they are only the basic minimum of people you will encounter in her house at any given time. Children, teenagers, and adults move freely in and out. One will receive a meal, another a haircut, a third a cup of coffee. She is a woman with the inner serenity that can come only from a deep commitment to Christ and daily communion with Him. This security communicates itself to others; and they seek her out for help with their problems, large or small. All seem to leave with their spirits renewed. She listens, laughs, and sometimes cries with them, gives food or counsel, or both. No one is in her house long without hearing about the Lord she serves, and many have given their lives to Him there.

If you have a teenager, you may find opportunities to minister to his friends. If they feel welcome in your home and sense that you accept them for what they are (or are not!), you will probably find yourself in the role of mother confessor sooner or later. So many young people cannot talk to their parents, or think they cannot, which amounts to the same thing; yet they feel a need for some wisdom that their peers are unable to give them.

Or perhaps you come in contact with teenagers even though you have none of your own. Your babysitter may have a problem that she would like to ask you about. If you are perceptive and open, she may tell you about it. I can remember two young brothers who took turns babysitting for us some time ago. We could hardly get them to leave when we got home, for it seemed as if they were just waiting for a chance to talk to us. They did not share any particular problems or difficulties, but simply seemed to need an adult who would really listen to them.

Fortify Your Efforts with the Word

There are people all around us who have no real friends—no one who cares deeply for their welfare. The average North American family moves every few years, often halfway across the continent. Relatives and friends are left behind. A woman who will open her home to those in need of friendship can perform a real service. We women are the world's helpers and healers; it is our special gift. In the same way that we comfort our husbands and children when they are distressed, we can lend a truly sympathetic ear to our neighbors and those around us. People with problems will eventually find someone to listen to them. But often the "helpers" they find are as needy as those they are trying to help. I know one woman who has made a mess of her own marriage and now tries to counsel her friends and neighbors who have marriage problems. Invariably she tells them, "You don't have to put up with that sort of thing. Just leave him." The more the unhappy wives air their gripes to her, the more justified they feel. To date, this "counselor" has been partly responsible for three divorces. We Christian women have so much good counsel to offer. If we are firmly grounded in Christ and are in the Bible daily, we can give the "word from the Lord."

This is where the importance of having many different Scripture passages at our fingertips shows up. A Christian psychologist, speaking to a group of pastors and wives on counseling, once said, "I cannot emphasize this one point too much; your success in counseling will be in direct proportion to the amount of Scripture that you have *in your head.*" He stressed the importance of holding the Scripture up as a mirror so that the people you are counseling can see themselves. I know from my own experience that I have been the most effective when I have been able to quote directly from the Bible while dealing with someone's problem. It is not necessary to be able to quote verses from memory, as long as you can find the appropriate passage and read it to the person. The Bible speaks to people with authority and power, whether or not they accept the validity of that authority. I have observed this time after time. A person will say that he does not know whether he believes in God or not, and he is not sure that the Bible is the Word of God. Yet when he has a problem and someone shows him what the Bible has to say about it he will, more often than not, accept it as authoritative. The Bible's power and effectiveness do not depend on man's recognition of it.

The Challenge of Being a Foster Home

Taking in foster children or adults can be another very effective way of using our homes to minister. Small babies often need homes before they can be given out for adoption. Many older children also need temporary homes, and these homes are usually in short supply. Taking in older children or teenagers should be accompanied with a vast amount of prayerful consideration, but it can be very rewarding. There are children whose parents are divorcing and neither one wants them. There are teenagers whose parents are unable to handle them. They are then labeled "incorrigible." (I am acquainted with one case like this in which it is obviously the parents who are "incorrigible," but the boy is the one who must leave home and be placed elsewhere.)

Almost all children who are placed in foster homes have emotional problems, by the nature of the case. It is important that anyone taking one of these children be prepared to cope with the problems. There must be a real commitment on the part of the foster parents. It may take quite awhile to establish communication. Perhaps for a time the parents' love will be rejected and their discipline resisted. If they give up in the face of these initial difficulties, the child is sent back and his sense of rejection and worthlessness is intensified. When a child is bounced from home to home, it does him more harm than good. These children are truly "the least of these" to whom Jesus referred. In ministering to them we are ministering to our Lord.

Raising foster children is not all difficulties of course. There is a beautifully bright side to the picture. Often they are so openly grateful for even the smallest courtesies that it is almost unbelievable. Some will quickly respond to the first unconditional love they have ever known. If in their previous homes affection was given when they were "good" and withheld when they were "bad," they were always under pressure to perform. Once this pressure is removed and they realize that someone really accepts them with no strings attached, a beautiful change is begun.

In the July 31, 1970 issue of the *Banner*, Carolyn Timmerman tells of taking in a young man who was facing dismissal from college because of discipline problems. After the first week in her home he confided that this was the first time anyone had ever bothered to say "good morning," "good night," or greet him politely in any other way. He since has become chairman of the honors committee of a large eastern university. She writes, "But we cherish the slat of the bed on which he slept, for years later when we happened to take the bed apart, we read, 'Thanks, thanks! 134 glorious days!' "

Friends of ours took in a foster daughter when she was a sullen, uncommunicative girl of thirteen. They went through a great deal with her. At one point she became obsessed with the idea of finding her real mother, who had abandoned her. Our friends patiently accompanied her on her rounds of the city's flophouses and dead-end bars until they finally found her mother. But it was to no avail. She refused to come home to her children. This was not the only crisis they weathered with their young charge. There were ill-advised love affairs, one resulting in a suicide attempt. The story has a happy ending, however. The foster parents were able to lead her to Christ as well as lend her their stability. She since has finished her studies to become a registered nurse, married a Christian young man, and presented our friends with their first "grandchild." She is now a wonderful wife and mother, and an asset to the community in which she lives.

Koinonia and Hospitality

Hospitality is also important within the church. We hear a lot about *koinonia* (spiritual fellowship) nowadays. This has always been an important part of the life of the church. Opening up of Christians' homes has played a part in this spiritual fellowship in the past and still plays a part today. There are occasions when the use of a church building is necessary and proper; but there are also times when a group can meet more effectively in a home, or a series of different homes. There are some cottage groups that meet for Bible study, discussion, and prayer whose success is partly due to the fact that they meet in homes.

Simply inviting a few people of the church over at a time for coffee and dessert is a good way to set the stage for spiritual communication and sharing. Sunday evening is often a good time for this, although it can certainly be another evening as well, if it works out better. A good way to begin is by inviting those church people who have never been in your home before, or those whom you know the least.

When you are doing this, be sure to include the single people: those who have never married as well as those who no longer have mates. It is important that these people be included in mixed gatherings. We have noted that man and woman together reflect the image of God. Besides complementing or completing each other physically, they also need each other intellectually, emotionally, and spiritually. So although men and women obviously need each other in marriage, the complementing of men and women is by no means limited to marriage. In the ordinary give and take of conversations and discussions, each sex can contribute something unique to the other.

Our sexuality is much broader and richer than we often suppose. It goes beyond its physical aspects. We all realize that a marriage includes much more than a physical union, that the physical aspect is, in a sense, an expression of the meeting of minds, hearts, and spirits. We must begin to meet some of the spiritual, emotional, and intellectual needs which single people have *as men and women*, as sexual beings. Many widows have told me that one of the hardest aspects of their single life is that they so seldom get to talk to a man. Women invite them, if at all, only for tea with other women or to all-women functions. These widows are not flirts or sex-starved in the way the phrase is commonly used. But they do need fellowship and communion with men. We who are married can go a long way toward alleviating their problems if we will simply include them in our mixed groups. Five or seven people can converse quite as nicely as four or six. We have been made aware that *koinonia* must transcend barriers of race, sex, and social class. It must also transcend the barrier of marital status.

Giving parties can be another effective way to practice hospitality. Some women have a special flair for this sort of thing. One of my prayer partners is an example. Her qualifications include a spacious home, a degree in home economics, and seemingly boundless energy. She loves to make all manner of fancy cookies, candies, and decorated cakes. Her cakes are all originals, each one exactly right for the occasion. Whether it is a shower for an expectant mother, a Christmas luncheon, or an afternoon tea; the food, the decorations, and the atmosphere are just right. And all of this is done within the framework of the Biblical idea of hospitality. She is not paying her social obligations; a great many of her guests have never entertained her and probably never will. She is simply giving different people in the church an opportunity to relax and have a good time together; to share another aspect of each other's lives as Christians. She is contributing her share toward building up the common life in Christ.

Of course a woman need not have a degree in home economics to be a successful party hostess! If that were the case there would be very few parties given. Nor is a large house necessary. Some of the most successful parties I have attended have been in a small room where most of the guests had to sit on the floor. In our first years of married life I served coffee to guests from an assortment of odd "cups" including pyrex custard dishes. Nobody minded.

There is room for a great deal of flexibility in the

way each of us practices hospitality. The important thing is that we begin to do it; for with the doing will come greater ease and delight, as well as rich rewards from our Master whom we serve also in this manner.

CHAPTER 5

Child-Raising: Off to a Good Start

Like Topsy who just "grow'd," children will usually grow into adulthood if they are reasonably well fed, have suitable clothes to wear, and are sent to school regularly. However, the kind of adults they will become (and indeed the kind of children they are right now) is, by God's order of things, largely up to their parents.

If we neglect our parental role, our children will take their direction from their peers. Many young people have no sense of direction today because they have been left to find guidance from their friends, who in all probability have no more wisdom than they. As one young teenager confided to her mother, "I'm glad I can talk to you when I have a problem. My friends just have to ask *their* friends, but how can that help? Their friends don't have any more experience that they do." Sadly, children who learn mostly from their playmates and buddies are still seeking direction in the same way when they are grown. They are the adults who make decisions on the basis of what people around them think. They lack the wisdom and courage to make decisions based on God's will.

Mothering in the Early Years

In our culture the larger share of child-raising falls to mothers. Fathers also have a vital role. This should not be minimized. In fact, the more time the mother spends with the children, the larger their horizons become, the more the father's role is also expanded. The father is responsible for the discipline and instruction of his children. This is his obligation and privilege. But since fathers usually are unable to be with their families for most of the day, the mother must assume the day-to-day care of the children. Encouragingly, God planned it that way, at least for the first years of a child's life, since women are created both to bear the children and nurse them. Of course technology has given us baby bottles—a mixed blessing, according to many doctors and dentists! (Breast-feeding, long out of favor, has recently become popular again. Interestingly, in the past mostly lower-class, poorly educated women nursed their infants, but today college-educated women are setting the trend. Also, they are the ones proclaiming the joy of childbirth.)

Intensive research by specialists in child care shows that the quality of mothering a child receives in his first six years is crucial. In the May, 1971 *Woman's Day* in her article "Raising a Bright and Happy Child," Myrna Blyth says, "... a mother is not only her child's first teacher; she may be his most important one as well." She concludes that the shape and scope of a child's intellect is largely in his mother's hands.

In the September, 1970 *Redbook*, Dr. Spock writes, "There is no doubt that the personality of a child is more pliable in his ... (early) ... years, and that during those years he constantly is being molded by his mother or by the substitute who spends the greatest amount of time with him."

This means that we mothers not only give birth to our children—we can give them life. The more time we are willing to spend with our children individually, the larger their imaginations can become, and the more creativity they will develop. They will become bigger persons.

In the November, 1970 *Redbook*, Dr. Spock continues, "A group of medical students and I were discussing the boredom that some mothers feel with child rearing. A woman in the group said that she would find it boring too. I asked her whether she would find the practice of child psychology boring, since it involves long hours of isolation with a series of difficult children each day. 'Of course not,' she answered. I asked, 'Why not?' 'Because,' she answered in an impatient voice, 'the psychiatrist is trying to *accomplish* something.' From my point of view a good mother is in a position to accomplish at least as much as a psychiatrist, and the job should be at least as gratifying."

The specialists affirm that a person's potential, both for emotional health and intellectual achievement, is determined in his childhood years. The Bible says the same for spiritual development. Proverbs 22:6 reads, "Train up a child in the way he should go, and when he is old, he will not depart from it" (RSV). Ephesians 6:4 instructs us to bring our children up "in the discipline and instruction of the Lord" (RSV). This, of course, implies that we know the Lord's discipline and have ourselves been instructed by Him. We cannot give what we do not have, or teach what we have not learned.

Importance of Parents' Personal Devotional Life

How can parents be sure that they are qualified to bring their children up in this way? The answer is really quite simple. It is also an old answer. The author of Psalm 119 knew it well. To understand God's will both for their lives and their children's, they must listen to God's Word. To achieve the kind of relationship with the Lord that is worthy of being taught and caught, they must be in the Scriptures daily, and alone. The same is true of prayer. Family devotions are very important. But this is something quite different. I am speaking here of the half hour or hour a day (or perhaps just ten minutes) spent alone with God. If you have not yet started this practice, begin now. Start with a few minutes, at the same time each day. For me it is the time when the older children have left for school and the youngest is watching Captain Kangaroo. Perhaps for some it will be during the baby's nap.

Start with a brief prayer that you will be open to the Spirit as you read. Then read a Bible passage; think carefully about what it says. Pray again, thanking God for the message you received and asking for wisdom to do something about it. As you continue each day, you will find yourself reading larger passages and praying about many things and for many people. A prayer list is helpful: it will aid in organizing your thoughts when you sit down to pray. You can jot items down during the day as you think of them. As you progress in your devotional life, you will find yourself sharing Biblical insights and answers to prayer with your children. You will be leading them into the abundant life which Christ talks about in John 10:10.

Children are great imitators. They imitate their friends, their older brothers and sisters, and especially their parents. We think it is cute to see a two-year-old carrying a make-shift briefcase "like daddy does." Sometimes we are a bit embarrassed when we hear some not-so-cute words coming out of his mouth that first came out of ours. Small children are not very discerning. It would be nice if they would copy only the good things we do. But alas, it does not work that way.

Paul tells the Philippians in chapter 3:17, "Keep on imitating me, brothers, all of you. We have set the right example for you." We do not have to urge our children to imitate us. They do this naturally. So it is up to you to be the kind of person you want your children to become. You must be worth imitating. If your religion is mostly a matter of performance—an emphasis on being a good, moral person—your children will learn to perform well. If instead they see a vibrant, personal relationship with Christ, this is what they will learn. A three-year-old neighbor of ours regularly takes a storybook and goes into a corner to have her "devotions." She does not really understand what this means, of course. She is simply play-acting at what she sees her mother do. But she senses that it is important, so she does it too.

The groundwork laid in the early years is a steadying influence during adolescence. But mothering is by no means ended now. Often in the later childhood years, when the adult is emerging, the challenge of being parents is the greatest. When children are small it is relatively easy to control them since, quite simply, their parents are bigger than they are. If the parents lack authority it is not noticeable. But parents no longer have physical superiority over adolescents.

Now it becomes very obvious that something else is necessary. What is needed is the authority of the Word of God. When you are daily looking for and following God's will for your own life, you are then able to lead your children to find God's will in the various daily decisions they must face. This requires from you a relationship with the Lord and with others that is totally honest and straightforward. Teenagers, particularly, sense hypocrisy very quickly. When they become aware of any phoniness, parental authority is seriously undermined. At this point many parents lose their children. These parents cannot speak with the authority of a personal knowledge of and surrender to the Word of God, and teenagers are too big to be spanked. Consequently, young people see no further reason to listen to their parents. As Joel Nederhood puts it in *The Holy Triangle*, "One of the main reasons parents have given up on the

69

training of their children is that they aren't sure of themselves anymore. They don't know God, and they don't know Jesus Christ, and they do not have the Holy Spirit in their hearts. They do not have any real convictions about what life is all about. They themselves have never come to grips with the biggest issues of life. They don't know what they are and they don't know who God is." [9]

Covenant Promise and Responsibility

Deuteronomy 6:6-9 says, "You must think constantly about these commandments I am giving you today. You must teach them to your children and talk about them when you are at home or out for a walk, at bedtime and first thing in the morning. Tie them on your finger, wear them on your forehead, and write them on the doorposts of your house!" (Living Bible). The covenant promise is given because God expects you to mold your children. This is your part of the covenant. You must personally communicate your faith to your children. By your daily walk with God and by sharing your knowledge of and experience with Him, God brings your children into maturity in His kingdom. God does His part. He never breaks faith. But so often parents do.

In *The Holy Triangle*, Dr. Nederhood continues, "Most of our young people are not rebelling against *Christianity* at all. They have just never been introduced to it by their fathers and their mothers." [10] We must spend time with our children, telling them what God has done in *our* lives and showing them how to find His will in their own lives. When the people were told in Deuteronomy 6 to teach the Lord's commandments to their children, it was in the context of *what the Lord had done for them*. Verses 20-25 read, "When your son asks you in time to come, 'What is the meaning of the precepts, statutes, and laws which the Lord our God gave you?' You shall say to him, 'We were Pharaoh's slaves in Egypt, and the Lord brought us out of Egypt with his strong hand, sending great disasters, signs and portents against the Egyptians and against Pharaoh and all his family, as we saw for ourselves. But he led us out from there to bring us into the land and give it to us as he had promised to our forefathers. The Lord commanded us to observe all these statutes and to fear the Lord our God; it will be for our own good at all times, and he will continue to preserve our lives.' "

The Israelites were not handing down a sterile set of dogmas and rules to their children which the children would find arbitrary and doctrinaire. The parents were to tell the children what the Lord had done for them and what the Lord would continue to do as long as they kept their end of the bargain.

You too, must put your teaching of God's commandments into the context of what God has done and will continue to do in *your* lives. Otherwise this teaching will seem to your children to be either irrelevant and unnecessarily restrictive, or, at best, rather quaint. And the results are predictable. A friend of mine in college sadly told me that she had lost her faith. She had been raised in a "Christian" home but now she simply could not believe. She had told me on other occasions that she had never in her twenty years heard her parents pray aloud. They had never led their children in prayer or talked to them of their faith. The parents had given their children the Lord's commandments, all right. They knew the rules and precepts. But the commandments were not given in the context of what God had done in their lives. No wonder this girl "lost" her faith. Very likely she never had it.

You do not have to simply "hope" that your children will be saved. You can give them the assurance of faith immediately. Recently I was in a conversation with several people that included a five-year-old. We were excited because a friend had just made a commitment to Christ. Since the five-year-old had been referring to herself as a Christian, someone asked her how long she had been one. She thought a minute and then solemnly answered, "I guess I've been a Christian all my life." This child is growing up in a family where the parents and older brothers and sisters freely talk about their faith.

Psychologists tell us that a person will, to a large extent, live up to what is expected of him. Certain things are "programmed" into all of us. If you consider your children as Christians, you will be expecting them to develop a personal relationship with Christ. This is certain to have a profound affect on them.

Genesis 17 tells us of the covenant that God established with Abraham. "God said, 'I make this covenant and I make it with you.' You shall be the father of a host of nations. . . . I will make you exceedingly fruitful; I will make nations out of you and kings shall spring from you. I will fulfil my covenant between myself and you and your descendants after you, generation after generation, an ever-lasting covenant, to be your God, yours and your descendants after you. . . . For your part, you must keep my covenant, you and your descendants after you, generation by generation." From the beginning in the community of believers the children were included. Throughout, the Bible emphasizes families of believers. The census of the people was taken by families. Blessings and punishments came to whole families. For example, Aaron's family received the honor of being priests. Achan, on the other hand, was killed for his sin, and his family was killed with him (Joshua 7).

Peter reiterates the covenant at the beginning of the New Testament church in his Pentecost sermon by quoting from the Genesis 17 passage. " 'Repent,' said Peter . . . and be baptised . . . in the name of Jesus the Messiah for the forgiveness of your sins; and you will receive the gift of the Holy Spirit. For the promise is to you and to your children, and to all who are far away, everyone the Lord our God may call' " (Acts 2:38, 39). God's promise is still both to believers and their children. Nowhere does the New Testament exclude children from God's promises and blessings. When the Philippian jailer believed "he and his whole family were baptised" (Acts 16:33, 34).

Misconceptions about Baptism and Nurture

One can readily see why some Christians have rejected infant baptism. They meet a great many young people who have been baptized as infants and ever after say, "I am Reformed," "I am Lutheran," or "I am Catholic," but there is no evidence in their lives of any kind of living relationship with Christ. This causes Christians who are serious about their faith to question the validity of infant baptism. Just recently my husband was approached by a woman who wanted her baby baptized "because he has some sins that have to be washed off." This mother had no intention of going to church or living in God's will. She merely wanted to go through a little ritual which she supposed would work a bit like a good-luck charm. This kind of thing is a gross misuse of baptism. God's covenant has two parts. Both parts must be kept for the covenant to be in effect. God will keep His, and believing parents must keep theirs. Talk of your faith with your children constantly. Baptism without nurture is like faith without works—dead.

There are several ways in which parents can go in a wrong direction in bringing up their children. Some trust in baptism by itself to make Christians of their children.

Others, going a step further, think that the church, Sunday school, catechism classes and Christian schools alone will do the job. They believe that education is the means of salvation. They try to educate people into the Kingdom. But they minister to the head only, not to the heart. This is sometimes carried to the extreme. Young people have on occasion been granted adult mem-

73

bership in the church as soon as they had mastered a certain amount of information. It was then assumed that they were Christians; no one really asked them about a personal relationship with Christ.

Nowadays this is not so likely to happen. Young people are taking a second look at what their parents are trying to give them. They are no longer satisfied with mere head knowledge, as some of their parents may have been. They call this kind of religion irrelevant and phony. No matter how logical it is, how beautifully it fits together, it does not fill their basic needs. Parents like these are presuming to claim their children for God without keeping their part of the bargain. They are trusting in the covenant to save their children without a real knowledge of what the covenant demands.

Still other parents dare not take God at His word with regard to their children. They look at them as non-Christians, just like children of unbelievers. They pray a lot for their children and "hope" that they will become Christians. Meanwhile they just watch for some sign that their children have been converted. I have known mothers who try to get their children to evangelistic meetings so that hopefully they will be saved. They seem to think there is nothing else they can do.

Some Christian parents, perhaps the largest group, combine all these attitudes together. They present their children to be baptized, they go to church and bring their children with them, they see to it that they get religious education, and they pray for them continually. These things are good; indeed, they are very important. Do not neglect them. There is no way, for example, that you can expect your children to grow as strong Christians if you are doing other things when you should be attending worship services, or if you neglect Christian education. But this still is not enough.

Proper Christian nurture demands that you talk to your children about what the Lord has done and is doing for you "when you are at home or out for a walk, at bedtime and the first thing in the morning." Then your children will respond with their own faith and commitment on their own level of understanding. You will not have to hope and pray that they will be saved someday. Like the five-year-old who "always was a Christian," they will be growing up in the kingdom. This is God's gracious and glorious covenant! As Dwight Henry Small says in *The Biblical Basis for Infant Baptism*, "Titus 1:6 teaches that a man qualifies to be an elder in the church when among other conditions, he has 'children that believe.' God expects the children of believers to be believers too! ... God is working on the sure principle that when Christian parents fulfill their covenant obligations on behalf of their children, those children will not only know and understand the gospel, but will have the grace of God to believe. The mark of a true Christian family, a true Christian parenthood, is that the children by proper training in the things of God will become Christians too. It is one thing to believe that one's children will eventually be saved; it is another thing to have confidence that one's children will grow up as true believers because of the faithful covenant-keeping of Christian parents. This verse teaches by implication what so many other passages teach, that when parents earnestly train their children according to the Word of God, God will honor them by giving those children grace to believe." [11]

Finding God's Will

An effective way to help your children grow in grace is simply to ask in different situations, "What do you think God wants you to do?" or "What does Jesus want you to do?" Then they can begin, while still very young, to find God's will for their own lives. This approach has the beauty of avoiding a contest of wills between the parent and child. The parent is acting not only on his own authority, but also pointing the child to the higher authority. And it is even different from "the Bible says" or "God wants you to" because the child himself is learning to respond to the Lord on his own level.

It is important not to make such statements as, "What would Jesus think if you did that?" because this tactic is judgmental. The child may then feel guilty or resentful. When he simply asks, "What does God want?" he finds power to act. He learns to become what sociologist David Riesman calls "inner-directed." He will govern his actions not by what people around him think, but by the inner strength and resources that God gives him. Children do not have the strength to withstand group pressures on their own. They are by nature the biggest conformists of us all.

A story about a third grader of my acquaintance illustrates this point very well. One of this little girl's classmates had a problem. His mother and father were both at work during the day, so he would come home to an empty house. One day he started playing with a cigarette lighter. He lit the doily covering the arm of the sofa and set the house on fire. After that everyone at school ostracized him. They called him "smelly Cornelly." When he would take his lunch to a table to eat, the others would get up and move away. My little friend came home and told her mother about this. She explained that Cornell was not one of her friends. She did not even think he was a very nice little boy. But she was quite upset about the way the children were treating him. She was wondering what could be done about it. Her mother said, "Janie, what do you think Jesus wants you to do about it?" She went into another room to think about it for a minute. Then she came back and said, "Mother, I think I know what Jesus would like me to do. I think He'd like me to take my lunch and go up and sit with Cornell." Her mother said she thought she was right. Janie asked, "May I take my sister along?" Her mother told her that would be fine. So the next day the two of them sat with Cornell at lunch. The following day a few others joined them, and in about a week the children had accepted Cornell again. Janie had found the power to risk being ostracized herself, to withstand pressure from her peers.

CHAPTER 6

Child Raising:
How To Apply Love and Discipline

Two things are of prime importance in raising children in "the way they should go": love and discipline. The two are really very much intertwined: if you truly love a child you will discipline him, and proper discipline must be carried out in love.

The Bible does not primarily regard love as an emotion: it is not first of all something one feels. The Bible speaks of love as an act of the will. In several places believers are *commanded* to love. II John 5, 6 reads, "Do not think I am giving a new command; I am recalling the one we have had before us from the beginning: let us love one another." One cannot produce an emotion on command; obviously a feeling is not what is meant. The love that God has for us, the love that we are to have for others, is a total, unconditional acceptance. The classic chapter on love, I Corinthians 13, says it beautifully.

In *The Art of Loving,* Erich Fromm says, "To love somebody is not just a strong feeling—it is a decision, it is a judgment, it is a promise. . . . A feeling comes and it may go. How can I judge that it will stay forever, when my act does not involve judgment and decision? . . . love is exclusively an act of will and commitment." [12]

Love Never Fails

Your children must know that your love is forever, whenever, and with no strings attached. Although you are expecting them to live the kind of lives that God wants them to live, they must know, without a shadow of a doubt, that if they should fail, you would still accept them. Unconditionally. This is something that should be put into words so that your children have no doubt about it. *You* know that you will always love them, but you *must be sure* that your children fully understand this. You must tell them that no matter what might happen, their home and parents are ready to take them back. The most terrible sins they could commit, the worst trouble they might get themselves into could never change the fact that they are your children and your home is their home.

One of our daughters, when quite small, used to worry about this. She has always had a high consciousness of her own sin, and she was afraid that she might someday be put in jail for something she might do wrong. We explained to her that if she possibly did anything that would put her in jail, she would still be our daughter and we would love her and accept her just as much as if it had never happened. We told her that God never stops loving us, no matter what we do, and we as her parents would never stop loving her either. She became assured of this and stopped worrying about the possibility of going to jail.

Parents who have just become Christians or who have only recently begun living the way God wants them to, may find that their children do not want to go along with their new life-style at first. The children may be indifferent or openly rebellious. In this situation, it is important to keep showing them love—to let them know that their parents' acceptance of them does not depend on their behavior conforming to this new standard. They may feel themselves to be in an unfair position: the rules of the game have changed overnight. What used to be an acceptable style of life suddenly is not. Children in this situation need the assurance that their parents love them and accept them the same as ever. In fact, they are now able to truly love them because of the love that Christ has given them. When the children understand that their parents' love is not conditional—that it does not depend on their "being good"—they will feel free to explore the possibility of following the faith of their parents.

Spending Time with Your Children

We must undertand what love really is, because we may not always *feel* loving and warm toward our children. But we can love them anyhow. We *must* love them anyhow.

But love demands many things from us. One of the most important things it demands is time. We must give of *ourselves* to give love, and this takes time. It cannot be worked in at odd moments. Each child needs his mother alone, preferably for some time each day.

How you spend your time with your children will depend on your abilities and the needs of each child. One thing that every mother can do is read to her children. Children love to be read to, and this is vital for their intellectual stimulation. Even older children who read well, still enjoy hearing stories read.

Two of our children are avid shoppers. They take turns accompanying me, whether it is for groceries, clothes, or anything else. They keep careful track of whose turn it is to go along. Another one loves to walk with me on my daily mile.

Special excursions occasionally with each child by himself also are important. It can be a trip to a museum, or something as simple as a sandwich shared in a nearby park. A milk shake together on a shopping trip can be very special. Or schedule time for talking together with your child alone in your room. Make it clear that no one is to disturb you while you have your time alone. Our youngest calls this her "privacy" with me. She is impatiently waiting for her legs to be long enough to keep up with me on my fast walks. Until then we have our "privacy" at home.

Physical Expressions of Love

An aspect of loving our children that should not be overlooked is the physical aspect. Children need hugging, cuddling, kissing—what some psychologists call "stroking." Psychologists now realize that babies can die simply from lack of cuddling. In past years some babies died in orphanages even though they were well-fed and were not physically ill. Today every effort is made to place babies in homes where they will receive love, as soon after birth as possible. In *I'm OK—You're OK*, Thomas Harris notes, "Stroking, or repetitious bodily contact, is essential to (the infant's) survival. Without it he will die, if not physically, then psychologically." [13] Touching a child says "I love you" in a way that nothing else can.

Most of us naturally fondle our babies, but often when the children grow a little older we stop doing this. Obviously ways of caressing our children will change as they grow older, but children do not outgrow their need for being touched. A rocking-chair is necessary equipment in a house where there are children. I rocked and sang to all of our children before bedtime until they were about five years old. I still rock them at different times

82

when they need that kind of comforting. Even our twelve-year-old daughter will occasionally want to be held and rocked in a "crisis" if I suggest it. It has a very calming, soothing effect on a distressed child. Physical expressions of love can be a great source of strength to children. Touching, however, should not be reserved only for occasions when a child needs comforting. And it should not stop when they are too old to be rocked. Teenagers need to be hugged, too.

It is interesting that in the youth sub-culture there is a great deal of touching on all levels. There is explicit sexual caressing, but there is also a lot of touching which simply expresses friendship. They throw their arms around each other's shoulders, touch hands, or link arms. Possibly as children they were not shown enough physical love by their parents, and they had to look elsewhere for it. It is likely that some of the promiscuity among the young is simply the expression of a need to be touched.

One reason sensitivity groups that involve touching have had good reception is because all but certain forms of touching are taboo in our society, and people crave this kind of communication. Although some sensitivity groups degenerate into wrong expressions, they are meeting needs that have not been met elsewhere.

All my children still get "tucked in" at night. I talk with each child individually before she goes to sleep. We talk about any problems that may have come up during the day, and then we pray together.

Discipline

Ephesians 6:4 tells us to bring up our children "in the discipline and instruction of the Lord." What does proper discipline involve?

Children crave discipline. They may protest, but they feel unloved when their parents are not disciplining them properly. I remember listening to the story of a man who had been apprehended on a manslaughter charge.

He told about his childhood. From the time he was very small he was allowed to roam the streets at night and get in whenever he pleased. No one ever asked him where he went. Every night he would go out, but he told us wistfully that he always wished someone would tell him that he had to stay home. He felt that his parents really did not love him, or they would not just let him do what he wanted. He felt no one cared.

What struck me was the fact that he felt compelled to go out every night until all hours, even though he did not usually enjoy it. How many children are getting into trouble doing things they do not even enjoy, simply because their parents have given them no regulations, no structure for their lives? Discipline shows our children that we care.

Discipline, like love, also takes time. Often a problem child—one that you "can't seem to do anything with"—is simply a result of not taking the time to follow through with discipline. It is easy to tell a child to do something and then leave it at that. Too often a parent threatens dire consequences if orders are not obeyed, but the parent is not prepared to carry out the threats. Take the time to give only reasonable, well-thought-out orders, and then follow through. Expect your children to obey you, and take the time and effort necessary to see that they do.

We cheat our children if we do not take the trouble to see to it that they obey. A young man, who had served time in prison for several offenses and had been in and out of jails for most of his adult life, was telling about his earliest delinquencies. When he was caught in his first misdemeanors his parents covered up for him. "I was lucky," he told me. But as soon as he said it he stopped and added, "Maybe I wasn't so lucky, at that." He realized that his parents' leniency had not been a favor. Because obedience had never been demanded from him, he had gone on to bigger crimes for which he was finally caught and punished.

Mistakes Are Not Disobedience

A child should not be punished for mistakes, only for disobedience. If a broken dish brings on the same spanking or verbal lashing as telling a lie, the child will equate mistakes with sin. One of our children, a very active child, went through a time when it seemed she was always knocking into, spilling, or breaking something. I became annoyed with these accidents and scolded her. Finally I realized that she had come to believe that breaking a dish or spilling a glass of milk was a sin. I had burdened her with a load of false guilt. When I realized this I stopped scolding about mistakes. When she understood the difference she was a much happier child.

Dangers of Permissiveness

The aim in discipline is to help our children to grow into disciplined adults. Discipline must first be imposed from the outside over a period of years so that the young person will achieve an inner discipline. In contrast, permissiveness leaves children with no direction and no goals in life.

Lack of discipline is often an attempt to buy a child's love. Parents want to be "good guys" and so are afraid to stand up to their children. They want their children to like them, to be their pals. Friendship between parents and children, particularly teenagers, is beautiful. Sometimes a parent is the only friend a child can trust. But equals they are not; peers they cannot be. A teenager needs his mother and father to be just that—parents, not pals. In the end permissive parents lose their children.

Eli was such a parent. He failed to discipline his sons. The result was not only the Lord's anger; his sons were lost to him as well. God holds parents responsible for their children's behavior. I Samuel 3:13 says, "My judgment on his [Eli's] house shall stand forever because he knew of his sons' blasphemies against God and did not rebuke them. Therefore, I have sworn to the family of Eli that their abuse of sacrifices and offerings shall never be expiated."

Establishing Good Work Habits

Teaching a child to work is important in discipline. Good work habits that will last a lifetime must be learned early, and the only way to learn is by actually working. As soon as children are able to perform little chores around the house, they should be required to do so—not just to help mother, but because *they need to work*. I did not understand this clearly when my older children were small. I looked at their "help" in a very business-like way and decided that it would not be very helpful. It was easier and faster to set the table myself than to supervise their doing it. The same was true of the dishes. The children tended to spill water on the floor, ruining my wax job, and I would still have to clean the sink and counters after them. So I would often politely decline their offers of assistance. I now realize that teaching them to do these things properly is an important part of my job. Children must be taught how to work and be required to do a good job at the tasks assigned to them. I also learned that after a brief training period children can, indeed, help a great deal!

In this automated age it may take a little effort and imagination to find enough real chores for everyone, but it can be done. Each child has a bed to make and a room (or part of a room) to keep neat. Even vacuuming can be done by a child of nine or ten after he is taught how to use the vacuum cleaner. Dishwashers must be loaded and unloaded, and there are always some items that must by washed by hand. Wastebaskets must be emptied and garbage carried out. Children can do yard work. There is the lawn to water and mow and weeds to pull. A small vegetable garden can be a child's own project to give him a sense of real accomplishment. There are leaves to rake, and later, snow to shovel. In spite of drip-dry and wash-and-wear, there are still some items that need to be ironed. Children can learn to do the wash. All of these chores will take supervision, especially the first few times. It will require an investment of time and effort by the parent before skills are mastered by a child. You must be willing to instruct your children carefully so they can do their work properly.

Homemakers: Past, Present and Future

A mother who has girls has an opportunity to teach them all of the homemaking skills—cooking, baking, sewing, cleaning. But girls do not have a corner on these accomplishments! Boys also can benefit from learning the rudiments of cooking and baking. All children can be taught to sew on buttons and press their clothes, to say nothing of doing a load of wash.

Training a daughter to be a homemaker is a special joy. There is nothing like having a young, eager apprentice around while you work! By doing this you will enable your daughter to begin her career as a homemaker with the confidence that comes from knowing that one is qualified. It is possible to learn homemaking skills on the job, of course, particularly if one has an understanding husband. But this is becoming increasingly more difficult as the pressures on homemakers to leave their calling increase. The young wife who was not given a positive attitude toward homemaking from her mother and has not mastered the basic skills will quickly become frustrated and discontented. She then may turn her back on her real profession to take an outside job, not because she really feels called to it, but simply as an escape. As a result she may become even more frustrated, but feel there is no way out. So every day she runs away from the mess at home to her outside job, leaving the family to muddle along the best they can.

One mother of several teenagers had worked outside her home almost all of her married life. She was not happy. Several times she said that she wished she were a good cook or she wished she could manage money properly or she wished she could sew. She had never been able to live on her husband's income, and she could not cope with the housework, so in desperation she looked for other employment. But with two sizable incomes the family still was barely managing. They spent tremendous amounts of money on food. As I listened to this unhappy woman, I thought how important it is to equip our daughters to be homemakers. We can spare our daughters a lot of unnecessary frustration if we give them both the skills that are needed and a sense of pride in their profession of homemaking.

By taking the time to teach your daughter the basic homemaking skills, you are also enriching her heritage and making memories that she will carry with her all her life. When I teach my daughters how to make the chili my mother taught me, or show them how to make the muffins that have been a family favorite for several generations, I am helping them to claim their heritage. I am giving them a sense of belonging to something larger than they are. If you have no recipes that you learned from your mother, no matter. You can start a tradition.

Give your children a sense of the larger family to which they belong, particularly if they do not live near their grandparents and other relatives. A generation or two ago this was no problem. A young person would usually marry someone from his hometown or nearby, and settle down near both sets of relatives. Today all that is changed, and parents must often make an effort to give their children roots. Cooking a dinner or making a dress with mother's help will create a fund of little memories adding up to a very special childhood.

Teaching Financial Priorities to Our Children

One important subject for parents to get in the proper perspective for their children is money. Money and its use greatly affects all of our lives. Children's attitude toward money is profoundly affected by the example they are given in the home. If parents consider their money as belonging to the Lord, to be used as He desires, they will be giving proper direction to their children. If, on the other hand, the parents first satisfy their own wants, this is what the children will learn. Pressure from society is strongly in the latter direction. Christian stewardship becomes increasingly more difficult in this affluent society. Our younger children have been asked by their classmates whether we are poor, since our children wear hand-me-down (though still good) clothes, and save their lunch bags for re-use.

There is more than one principle involved here. First, it is wasteful and ecologically unsound to discard things that are still useful simply because of our craze for newness. We can no longer afford this either as a nation or as individuals. Even if our natural resources were unlimited, the disposal problem would demand that we change our ways. But even more important as a principle is the matter of setting priorities in the use of our money as in everything else. Whether or not we can "afford" an item may not be the only consideration. Money decisions must be made the same way other decisions are made—by asking what God wants. Money, like time and everything else, must be used in the Kingdom of God.

Stewardship begins with tithing. This was required of the Old Testament people of God who wandered around in tents and could see only the outlines of God's marvelous plan of salvation. They had neither the material nor the spiritual blessings which we enjoy. Surely we who live on the other side of the cross will want to give no less. If we are faithful in our giving, our children will learn this from us. And this helps to put the whole subject of money in its proper perspective.

One little boy, a son of a minister who served an affluent community, had playmates who lived in a style quite different from his family's. One day he came home and said, "Why doesn't Dad get a job where he can make a lot of money, too?" When his mother explained what their priorities were, he was satisfied. He understood that although the family could afford to buy what the other children had that he wanted, they had decided to use their money in ways they considered to be more important. He began to understand what his dad's commitment to Christ involved. Now that he is old enough to have a paper route and earn some money of his own, he is faithfully tithing. His parents never told him that he had to, or even specifically suggested it. He is simply following their example.

Bridging the Generation Gap

A generation gap is not built into a home where there are teenagers. When parents have spent time with their children from the beginning, sharing their faith with them, and giving them love and proper discipline, there will be no generation or communications gap. One teen-aged girl raised in such a home was asked to write an essay on "The Generation Gap." She honestly did not have any idea what to write. There simply was no such thing in her home. When parents and young people have the same aim—finding God's will for their lives—there cannot be a communications gap. Christians who let the Spirit lead them have no trouble communicating, no matter what their age, race, or status.

Adolescents have special problems and difficulties, of course. These are the years when they are trying to find out who they are and where they are going. Some feel compelled to solve most of the world's major problems singlehandedly. But crucial as all of these concerns are, they can be faced with equanimity by young people who are secure in their relationship with Jesus Christ and with their parents. If the parents have laid the groundwork, the children by this time will have a firm grasp on the faith of their fathers, and will have their own living relationship with Christ and a real commitment to Him.

Teenagers should be encouraged to participate fully in the life of the church along with their parents. This would include the Lord's Supper. Children who have made a profession of their faith at the beginning of adolescence (at twelve or thirteen) grow in faith by partaking of the sacrament and by knowing that they are accepted on an equal basis with other believers. This provides tremendous security at a time in their lives when they are often insecure in other areas. Socially they may feel "all thumbs"; intellectually they are trying to find themselves; emotionally they may be unsteady. If spiritually they are secure in their place in the church, the body of God's people, they can find the strength to cope with other areas of life without losing their balance. Young people need the communion of the saints as much as adults do. And they can make their contribution to the life of the church as well.

This does not mean that we are always to treat teenagers as adults. Parents often are told to trust their children, especially by their own teenagers. A son or daughter may ask accusingly, "Don't you trust me?"—perhaps hoping his parents will feel guilty and give consent to whatever he or she wants to do.

In *The Christian Family*, Larry Christenson writes, "... the intimidated parent should reply, 'of course I don't trust you, honey.' Trust is not something you dispense freely, like pink lemonade, to spread a feeling of togetherness. Trust is built on solid experience, not emotion. You would not think of 'trusting' your son—who has just finished a course in freshman chemistry and wants to be a doctor—to perform an operation. Your trust would be premature and altogether misplaced. To trust young people with the explosive potentials of sex (for instance)—throw them completely on their own, with no safeguards, rules, or restraints—is as foolish as thrusting a surgeon's knife into the hands of a pre-med student. This is not trust, but foolish and dangerous irresponsibility." Parents must set limits on their children's behavior until such a time as they have gained enough experience and wisdom to do so themselves.

Our two young teenagers are not allowed to date until a later time which we have decided upon. They have known and accepted this for quite some time. However, last year our oldest, then a freshman in high school, was asked to the Sweetheart Ball, *the* social event of the year. Somehow she thought that we would make an exception just this once. All her friends were going, she argued. (Quite true.) Just once wouldn't hurt anything. She would never ask again, etc. When it became clear that we were not going to relax our rule, she dissolved in tears and cried half the night. My husband and I knew we had done the right thing, but we still felt a bit like ogres. The next morning at breakfast she said that during her devotions, a text had come to her attention which had shown her that she would be given the right words to say to the boy who had asked her to go with him. She had fully accepted our decision; we never heard anymore about the matter. In fact, she reported that the young man told her he guessed he would just have to wait for her to be old enough.

Conclusion

Bringing up children is a tremendous responsibility, but God will equip you for the task. When you walk daily with the Lord and let His Word speak to you, when you have your priorities straight, you will be able to give direction to your children. You will be able to love them, discipline them, and help them find God's will for their own lives. You will be speaking of your faith to your children daily. As you do all of these things in working out your part of God's covenant, you can be sure He will not let you down. With complete confidence and thanksgiving you can claim your children for God.

CHAPTER 7

Money Matters

Getting Our Money in Perspective

Thrift is pretty much an outmoded concept today. In fact, the word itself has nearly disappeared from the language. However, it is an important part of stewardship. If we understand that all of our money and material possessions are really the Lord's and we are His stewards—His managers and supervisors of financial affairs here on earth—we will see how important it is that we manage well: that we are, in fact, thrifty. It is the Lord's money that is feeding and clothing our families, supporting the spread of the gospel, and caring for those in need. When we are not managing properly, it is the Lord's money that is slipping through our fingers. This is as serious a breach of trust as burying our talents.

It is encouraging to see that God gives us the ability to be good money managers when we are trusting Him and are serious about pleasing Him in this area. In the chapter on Child-Raising we saw the importance of tithing in teaching our children to set financial priorities. Tithing also helps families to be good money managers. It is not always clear whether the practice of tithing is in itself a discipline which sets the stage for further discipline in money-handling, or whether God gives greater financial blessings to those who trust Him in this way. Probably it is a combination of both.

Time after time families have told me that as soon as they started tithing—when they took a tenth of their income out for God first and trusted that they could live on the rest—they seemed to have more than ever before. They were actually living better on nine-tenths of their income than they had been on the whole of it. Some have experienced this in the form of raises in salary and unexpected bonuses. Others have said that for the first time they were forced to do some bookkeeping and set their financial affairs in order. They could not give a tenth until they figured out what a tenth was!

A life of stewardship is a life of faith. We are required to take God at His word, to trust the promise of Matthew 6:31-34, "How little faith you have! No, do not ask anxiously, 'What are we to eat? What are we to drink? What shall we wear?' All these are things for the heathen to run after, not for you, because your heavenly Father knows that you need them all: Set your mind on God's kingdom and his justice before everything else, and all the rest will come to you as well. So do not be anxious about tomorrow; tomorrow will look after itself. Each day has trouble enough of its own."

A pastor tells of a young couple he was counseling. He suggested that they consider tithing. Even though he had a job that paid well, the husband protested that they just did not have enough money to give to the Lord. The minister persisted, "Don't you think the Lord could take care of you on nine-tenths of your income?" "Oh yes," the young man assured him. "God is all-powerful. He can do anything." "Then why don't you trust Him and begin to tithe?" the pastor suggested. Immediately the young man flashed back, "*You* try to pay our bills on nine-tenths of my salary!" He trusted God in theory, but he did not have the faith to carry it out in practice.

There is no reason to stop with a tithe, of course. As the Lord blesses us financially and as we grow in faith we will want to go beyond the tithe, perhaps far beyond.

A Savings Plan

We have noted that the husband is responsible for taking leadership in setting financial priorities for the family. However, the wife has the responsibility of contributing her insights and talents in this area as elsewhere. One way in which she can be helpful is by suggesting that the couple put aside a certain amount of money on a regular basis. Some have proposed that, as a rule of thumb, ten percent of the family's gross income be put away each month. This may be too much for a family at times when expenses are heavy. At other times they may be able to save more. The important thing is to establish the habit of regular saving. It is all too easy to go through the entire paycheck each month. And it has been shown that the amount of income has very little bearing on whether people save or not. There are people at all income levels who are spending themselves into bankruptcy each year. They are spending more than they make, whether this be $6,000 or $100,000 a year. There are also people at these same income levels who consider that they live comfortably, and who are saving for a "rainy day." It is not the amount of income that is significant, but how it is managed.

Except in cases of extreme poverty or special emergencies, God is not pleased when His people live from paycheck to paycheck. People who can "afford" to buy things or do things on payday that they cannot afford on other days are letting their money run them. They

97

are not in control of their circumstances; their circumstances are controlling them. They have become the slaves of mammon as surely as the person whose consuming passion is to amass a fortune. And a person who is not in control of his money is not fulfilling his God-ordained role as steward.

The Homemaker's Financial Contribution

Even if her husband is not very responsible in handling money, a thrifty woman can be a tremendous help in keeping the family on an even keel financially. Over the years I have become convinced that a committed homemaker can make more of a financial contribution to her household than a woman working at almost any job outside the home. Even a woman with a fairly large salary can find that extra taxes, baby-sitter's fees, more clothes, and increased food bills take the lion's share of the second income. One of our friends told me recently that while his wife had a full-time outside job, he was beginning to suspect that the net gain in income was very little. For a few months he kept careful track of their expenditures. His conclusion was that after their extra expenses were met all that was left of her salary was twenty-five dollars a month. This is by no means an isolated example. I have heard similar stories from scores of couples.

One of my favorites concerns a young mother of two pre-schoolers who kept pleading that she had to keep her job "just until we get out of debt." They could not manage to keep a babysitter for the children. so they were shifted from one temporary place to another. The father worried that they were losing contact with the children. Finally, the mother was forced to quit her job, as she was expecting twins. Seven months later she sheepishly admitted to my husband that because she stayed home the family had gotten out of debt! She explained that she had started to do her own baking, and she began

to fix economical meals. She enjoyed cooking, and keeping
the cost low became a challenge to her. She also stopped
buying so many of the expensive cosmetics she had not
been able to resist when she saw them every day. There
were many other savings which she was able to make,
all of which added up to more than her previous earnings.

Keeping Track of Expenditures

As a full-time homemaker you can be "making money"
for the family in a variety of ways. The best way to
begin is to keep a list, for a month, of every penny
that you spend and where. Keep a small spiral notebook
in your purse for the purpose. This will help you to
see where your money is actually going. When you have
it laid out in front of you, you will be able to determine
which expenditures are for bare necessities, which are
for things that are good but not absolutely essential,
and which are just plain waste.

This kind of accounting can be very revealing. One
woman may find that she is dribbling a great deal of
money away on things which are very unimportant. Another may find that she is doing a pretty good job of handling her money. In any case, each will become aware
of areas that are potential problems for her. At this point
it is possible to set up a realistic budget for household
expenses. The expenses in the first category, that of
the fixed essentials, will remain. The second category
contains expenditures which are optional. Each homemaker will juggle these around to best suit her family's
needs. The last category, that of unnecessary spending,
should of course be eliminated altogether.

The Usefulness of a Household Budget

The word "budget" often intimidates people. Sometimes it even arouses feelings of hostility. A man once
told me, "My wife thinks 'budget' is a dirty word."
On the contrary, a budget is a tool which, like all tools,

is designed to help the person who is using it to do the job at hand. The proper tool is always necessary in order to do the best job. Some people find a very detailed budget serves them best; others can get by with only the barest outlines.

A wife will generally be responsible for making purchases in three categories: food, clothing, and housekeeping items. Of the three the food budget is the easiest to plan, since a family's food needs change quite gradually. Clothing purchases will vary not only with the season, but also somewhat from year to year. Sometimes it is possible to plan so that only one member of the family buys a new coat in a season, for instance, but at other times purchases seem to lump together. Household expenditures will also vary from time to time. For instance, a new vacuum cleaner may put a sizable dent in the housekeeping items' part of the budget. It is important to allow for such expenditures in one's long-range plan.

Planning and Shopping for Meals

The supermarket gets a big chunk of our money each week. There are many ways in which a homemaker can substantially reduce this amount. I am firmly committed to serving nutritious, well-balanced meals for as little money as possible. One good reason for saving money here is that every week the money spent for food is simply gone, with nothing left to show for it. At least when one splurges for, say, a good piece of furniture, it can be enjoyed for several years. Tonight's dinner, on the other hand, is simply tomorrow's garbage.

How can one significantly reduce food bills without sacrificing nutrition? Careful menu-planning and shopping are the answer. These are two things that the woman with an outside job seldom has the time or energy to do. Studies have shown that wives working outside the home spend up to twice as much for food as those who remain at home. Many money-saving meals, although not more difficult to make, require preparation well before mealtime. Dried beans must be soaked overnight; home-made soups and stews should simmer several hours. Expensive steaks and chops cook very quickly; meat loaves and pot roasts take longer. Less expensive meals need not be any less pleasing. My family's two favorite dishes are two of the cheapest to prepare.

To be a careful grocery shopper one must be knowledgeable. The first requirement for this is to memorize the prices of all the items one buys regularly. This cannot be done overnight, of course. The best way is to start with the most frequently purchased articles and move on to the others. This is the only way to know whether an advertised "special" is a bargain or not, and if so, how much of a bargain. There are some items that one need never buy at the regular price. For instance, I have not paid the regular price for tomato soup for several years. Whenever it is on sale, I buy a flat or two and store them, since tomato soup is the base for many of our favorite dishes.

Buying large quantities of necessities when they are on sale seems an obvious way to save money, yet I find that many housewives do not do this on a regular basis. Some have a mistaken notion that this kind of buying requires a greater outlay of money. This is just not so. If you buy eight pounds of coffee one week, for example, it is clear that it will not be necessary to spend money on coffee for the next while. Perhaps the next week the price of chickens will be low enough so that you can buy several for the freezer. The next week the bargain might be eggs. (They will keep several weeks if they are refrigerated immediately.) And so on. There are, of course, a few items that never go on sale. But many items are substantially cheaper at certain times. Some things such as fresh produce, chickens, and eggs go by seasons. The prudent thing to do is to stock up on them and serve them often when they are most plentiful, and at the height of their flavor.

Another way to save money is to eliminate potato chips, soda pop, candy, and other "junk foods" from the food budget. Since these foods contribute almost nothing nutritionally except calories, they are very costly indeed.

Baking Saves Money

Someone has said, "In a family where there are children, there is no such thing as too many cookies." How right she was. And it is considerbly cheaper to make them at home than to buy them. The same is true of pies, cakes, bread, and other baked goods.

Money and Clothing

My favorite way of saving money on children's clothes is using hand-me-downs. The older ones pass their clothes on to the younger children in the family. But we have also received a lot of good, usable clothing from friends and neighbors over the years. Perhaps your situation is different. However, you can often buy good clothing at a fraction of its worth. Mentally run through the list of friends and neighbors who have children a little older than yours, and then ask them about selling the clothes their children have outgrown. In this way you can get clothes when they are still in fashion.

Savings on clothing bought at sales can often be enormous. Since you as a homemaker can plan your own schedule, you can usually manage to be at the best sales to get the bargains. Be sure to be at the store when the doors open. The really sensational bargain items are often sold out within minutes of opening time.

Sewing clothes is another way to "make money" as a homemaker. When you can manage to get the fabric on sale as well, your garment can be a spectacular bargain.

Savings on Household Items and Maintenance

There are many possibilities for saving money on household items. All you need is time and a little imagination. You can sew your own tablecloths and napkins. You can also buy a colorful sheet on sale to use as a tablecloth. This will cost considerably less than buying a tablecloth of the same size. Making draperies, curtains, and toss pillows are other money-saving possibilities for the home sewer. Refinishing secondhand furniture, painting walls, and hanging wallpaper are all ways in which to save money. You can do as many of these things as your time and inclination allows.

Services You Need Not Buy

An ever-increasing proportion of the American family's dollars goes for services each year. A thrifty homemaker can keep this amount down in a variety of ways. For instance, you can be the family barber. With the slightly longer hair styles it is not even necessary to use a clippers. A barber's shears or razor is all you need.

If babysitting is a big item in your budget, consider joining a co-op where members take turns sitting for one another. When my oldest children were small, I traded a few hours once a week with a neighbor. I needed the time to practice the organ. She used her hours to have time alone with each of her children in turn while I babysat the other two.

Babysitting is not the only thing you can trade. You may be able to work out your child's piano lessons by giving some other service in exchange. Perhaps you can trade some of your baked goods in return for the services of a friend who is good at hair-styling. There are a great many possibilities.

Thrift Brings Freedom

When the practice of thrift becomes an unconscious habit, it brings a great sense of freedom. First, there is freedom from financial pressures. As we have noted, money is probably the cause of more tensions and problems between husbands and wives than any other single thing. Without the practice of thrift there is never enough money, no matter how much the husband's income. The wife can add another income, but still there will not be enough. Proper money-handling can head off these tensions and so give a couple greater freedom in their marriage relationship. Also, thrift gives a family the freedom to do things that are very valuable but otherwise could not be managed, such as travel, and college education for the children. It also brings freedom from a nagging worry in the back of the mind about coping with a possible financial emergency.

Conclusion

Our money is given us by the Lord, to be used for Him. He is pleased when we are generous in our giving back to Him, and prudent in our use of it to meet our daily needs. This is proper stewardship.

CHAPTER 8

The Volunteer

Community Needs

Recently I was talking to the director of the Camp Fire Girls in our area. She told me that because it is becoming increasingly more difficult to find mothers who will offer their services as group leaders, the organization may be forced to start hiring people to fill these positions. Scout leaders tell of similar problems. As our society becomes more complex, the need for volunteers multiplies. There is an exciting range of possibilities for serving the community in this way.

Biblical Mandate for Social Action

James 1:27 says, "The kind of religion which is without stain or fault in the sight of God our Father is this: to go to the help of orphans and widows in their distress and keep oneself untarnished by the world." This is by no means the first reference to orphans and widows in the Bible. It is a recurring motif in Scripture, both in the Old Testament and the New. Many of the prophets dealt with this theme. Isaiah 1:17 reads, "Cease to do evil and learn to do right, pursue justice and champion the oppressed; give the orphan his rights, plead the widow's cause."

In a pamphlet *The Biblical Basis for Christian Involvement in Social Concerns*, Dr. Douglas Stuart of Gordon-Conwell Theological Seminary points out, "The phrase 'orphans and widows' is used in many laws of the Old Testament. The two most abused members of society stand for *all* people who are oppressed or needy. The Scripture demands that the people of God be actively involved in the defense of and concern for these people." [14] We, the people of God, must be socially aware and concerned. We must actively serve the community in which He has placed us.

Flexibility of Volunteer Work

There are many ways in which we can serve individuals and groups who need our help. When our children are very small we probably will not want to become involved in projects that take us out of the house very much. As our children get older and are in school, we will find our schedules more flexible. One of the nice things about being a volunteer is that we are free to decide which tasks can best utilize our talents. We can also decide which hours we will work and how many. Our time can be scheduled so that we are at home when our families need us.

Ministering to the Sick and Shut-in

Almost any congregation will at any given time include at least one or two people who are hospitalized, chronically ill, or in a nursing home. We can see in these people an important opportunity for ministry. A visit from someone who really cares is a bright spot in any sick person's day. And older people or others confined to convalescent homes to live out their last years are often woefully neglected, much to our shame. Many of these people have very little contact with the outside world. Their only companions are the other inmates of the home. They are often particularly happy to see children. So if you have a pre-schooler, bring him along when you visit the nursing home. He will be most welcome.

It is not only those in our congregation who need visits, of course. There are others in the community who are ill and need our help. If the sick person or invalid is a wife and mother, her family needs help too. They may need help with meals. It is particularly nice to bring dinner the first day that she is home from the hospital after surgery, illness, or having a baby. This can ease the trauma of having to cope with a household again after hospitalization. There are other ways to help. Perhaps the house needs cleaning or the laundry needs to be done. Or perhaps offering to care for her children for part of the day while she naps would be the best way to serve.

Hospitals

Hospitals have a continuing need for volunteers. Hospital costs are at a staggering high. Unless we have extensive health insurance, few of us can afford to be hospitalized. And yet costs would be a great deal higher still if it were not for the services of all those who cheerfully and faithfully give of their time. In one of our local hospitals which has one hundred thirty-eight beds, volunteers donated twenty-six thousand hours of service and five thousand dollars worth of equipment last year. Without this help the hospital's standard of efficiency and service could not be maintained. This is true in hospitals all over the country. If all volunteers were suddenly to withdraw, there would be an immediate, drastic rise in rates and a possible crisis situation in patient care.

There are different ways in which hospital volunteers serve. There are strictly fund-raising activities as well as direct services for the patients. The list of these services is often quite varied, depending on the hospital. The hospital with which I am best acquainted offers its volunteers seventeen different types of service. A woman can sign up for any service for which she thinks she would be best suited. She might help with the library, bringing a cart with magazines and books to the patients' rooms. Or she might help staff the coffee shop. This is a real service to relatives and friends who are anxiously waiting for an operation to be completed, or a baby to be born. In some hospitals volunteers are even used to assist in the emergency room.

Education

Schools can do a better job of educating our children on their limited budgets when they have volunteer helpers. Homemakers can help in the library, on the playground, and in the classroom. Teacher's aides can correct papers, tutor children who need special help, and generally be an extra pair of hands for the teacher.

The classroom is not the only place where effective tutoring can take place. Many cities have private tutoring programs for disadvantaged children. One need not have a college education to qualify as a tutor. The real qualification is a willing heart. Many children who have "passed" one grade after another without ever learning to read have learned in a few months under a homemaker who had time to give them instruction on a one-to-one basis and who really cared about them.

Those in Prison

Convicts and ex-convicts are certainly numbered among the "least of these" with whom Christ indentifies himself in Matthew 25. Job Therapy, Inc., an organization which started in Washington State and has since spread to many other states, uses volunteers to help rehabilitate prisoners who previously had been considered unredeemable. A prisoner is given a sponsor who agrees to visit him or her at least once a month until he is released. (Preferably this is begun a year previous.) When that time comes the sponsor escorts his friend from prison and stays with him for his first full day back in society. He also helps him with the different problems that face him as he again takes his place in the community.

The idea for Job Therapy began with Richard Simmons, a concerned young citizen who began visiting young men in Washington State Reformatory. He was struck by the loneliness of the inmates. Often they received no visitors or mail; their families had rejected them. They became lethargic and bitter, nourishing their hatred of society.

Simmons began an intensive study of rehabilitation programs all over the world. The country that stood out was the Netherlands which boasted a ninety-percent success rate for ex-offenders, while the United States' success rate was only fifty percent. He figured out that if the State of Washington could match the Netherlands' record, they could have only three hundred seventy-five prisoners in maximum security instead of three thousand. The saving this would effect in lives and dollars was staggering. The key to the Netherlands' success was the use of thousands of private citizens as volunteer sponsors who made themselves available to the prisoners as real friends who were concerned with their morale and their future. These friendships began while the inmates were still in prison and continued after they were released.

The officials in Washington State were convinced and gave their approval for such a program of help on a one-to-one basis; Job Therapy was born. Its success has been most gratifying. Prisoners identify with their sponsors in a way they seldom do with prison counselors or chaplains. To date, the demand for sponsors is much greater than the supply.

There are many ways in which a homemaker can help in this program. In some instances she herself can sponsor a woman prisoner. If her husband is a sponsor she can go with him on visits, and invite the prisoner into her home when he is released. She can help the prisoner's wife to cope with the situation both during and after the husband's time in prison. The wife of a prisoner has problems which are unique to her situation. Her family may try to turn her against her husband, saying he is "no good." Her friends may desert her. And there is the special loneliness which even a widow does not experience: she is married, but in effect has no husband. A homemaker who has a good marriage and a stable family life can be a tremendous help to the prisoner's wife if she cares enough to give of herself. Among other things, she may be the only model this woman has of a good wife and mother.

The Environment

Preserving the environment is a field that is desperately in need of our aid. There is much to be done, and quickly. We homemakers are in a perfect position to help. Anthropologist Margaret Mead says in an article in the April, 1970 *Redbook*, "Women still are, as women always have been, caretakers of persons and equally, caretakers of the things that are essential to those they love and for whose well-being they are responsible. And it is just this—responsible and devoted caretaking—that is the key to the future. ... (women) must make a translation in terms from housekeeping for a family ... to housekeeping for all people." * In practical terms this can mean, for example, organizing recycling programs. At the fantastic rate we are presently using up our raw materials, including air and water, we can no longer afford to use things once and throw them away. Recently in one of our major cities, two women took it upon themselves

---

* Reprinted from *Redbook* magazine, April 1970. Copyright © 1970 by The McCall Publishing Company.

to convince the city's industries to use re-cycled paper. After they met with considerable success, they went on to spearhead a campaign to collect the paper on a continuing basis.

The Arts

In most communities there are various volunteer organizations devoted to the arts. These often include groups to help promote orchestral and choral music, drama, opera or light opera, and ballet. The manager of the symphony orchestra in our city has said that the orchestra could not exist if it were not for homemakers who give of their time to the orchestra and the symphony guild. She said, "Let's face it: If all the women in the area had full-time jobs outside the home, we would have to fold up." Which means that we women have a responsibility in guarding our cultural heritage.

Organized Help for the Helpless

Volunteer organizations of a different type from those we have known before have recently come into being. These are the "Good Samaritan" groups that are forming all over the country. Probably the best known of these good-neighbor groups is Fish, which started in this country less than a decade ago and has since grown to over a thousand chapters. Its name comes from the initials of the Greek words "Jesus Christ Son of God Savior." These initials spell *ichthus*, the Greek word for fish. Fish members provide a variety of services for those in need. They run errands for shut-ins, provide baby-sitting service in emergencies, bring in meals when a mother becomes ill suddenly, and generally do what they can to meet the needs that are brought to their attention. Members sign up in advance to be on call on certain days during certain hours. These hours can be arranged to fit the members' schedules. Anyone can be a Fish volunteer, but the homemakers of each community where it exists are its real backbone.

Homes for Juveniles

In an effort to help juvenile offenders, many communities set up detention centers. Young people are referred to these centers when they are in trouble of one sort or another. Sometimes it is for acts which would be defined as criminal if they were committed by adults; sometimes they have run away from home (our local chaplain tells me that by far the majority of girls referred to them are run-aways); often the parents cannot handle the child, so he is referred to the authorities. In these last cases, more often than not, the problem began with the parents who are themselves problems.

How does a homemaker who wants to help fit into this picture? She can offer her home as a temporary foster home. Some communities do not have the facilities to house youngsters in a detention home. In any case, most prefer to place them in stable homes in the community. They have found this to be much better for the young people. This may be only a matter of a day or two, although sometimes it can be weeks before the problem is straightened out. In almost every community there is a shortage of qualified homes. One of the requirements usually is that the mother not be employed outside her home.

Unwed Mothers

Since society's attitude toward unwed mothers has radically changed in the last couple of decades, homes for unwed mothers are not as common as before. But many communities still have them. If your community is one of these, your services as a volunteer will be welcomed. Again, you may be able to offer your home as

112

a foster home. Programs differ from place to place. Perhaps you will arrange to come in at certain times to teach the girls a skill, such as sewing, or meal-planning.

Often the downtown mission works with unwed mothers. You might be able to help by working into their program.

Christian Organizations for Teaching and Evangelism

There are many Christian organizations devoted to Bible study and evangelism which depend in large measure on volunteers to carry out their programs. Some of the ones that I am most familiar with are Young Life, Youth for Christ, Campus Crusade for Christ, Inter-Varsity Christian Fellowship, Navigators, and Bible Study Fellowship. This last, although beginning to have men's groups, is still largely a women's movement. Everywhere it exists it depends on volunteer discussion leaders. All of these organizations have a place for homemakers who are willing to help.

The Church

While we are discussing how we can serve within specific organizations, we should not forget the organizations within the church. We serve in different ways as people of God, ministering to those around us outside the framework of any specific organizations. But God's people are also called to serve in different structures of the church, such as the Sunday school, the choir, and various committees. There are certain vitally important aspects of the church's work that can only be done through these different groups. There are plenty of opportunites for homemakers to serve in this way. Most congregations are in need of Sunday school teachers. Rare is the church that always has a full quota of qualified teachers, including substitutes! The calling program in most churches can use some help. If you are not sure where you can be the most useful, your pastor will be glad to help you find and develop the gift God has given you.

Conclusion

The community needs us; the Bible commands us to help; organizations can provide the framework. (The organizations mentioned in this chapter are by no means the only ones that exist. They are only given as examples of the avenues through which homemakers can serve.) When we begin to see the broad range of possibilities open to us, we start to realize the excitement of it all. We women are indeed this planet's caretakers. God has, in large measure, put the culture of our generation and generations to come into our hands.

CHAPTER 9

Sharing Our Faith

Urgency of Spreading the Good News

Some years ago a visiting minister told a true story in his sermon that haunts me still. A young man returned to work on Monday morning all excited. Over the weekend he had attended a Billy Graham crusade and had become a Christian. He had worked for his employer for several years and the two were good friends, so he could hardly wait to tell him all about it. After he finished talking the employer said, "That's great, John! I'm a Christian too, you know." John answered, "You are! And all this time I thought what was the sense in becoming a Christian if a person could be as good as you are without being a Christian." By not telling others of his faith in Christ this employer was preaching humanism, or a kind of works salvation. Instead of leading his friend to Christ, he was actually blocking the way.

We homemakers are caretakers for the world. It is vitally important that we meet people's physical needs.

But if we are serious about helping people, if we are genuine in our concern for their well-being, we must go farther than this. As Dr. T. A. Raedeke, Executive Director of Key '73, said recently when he was in our city to speak, "If we don't personally confront people with the gospel of Jesus Christ and show them how they can commit their lives to Him, all our social concern does nothing but send them to hell with full stomachs." That is a very blunt statement, but perhaps a necessary one for many of us to hear. If we do not give our cup of cold water, *in the name of the Lord*, we are indistinguishable from the humanists.

All Must Witness

Witnessing is not an option for a Christian. Christ did not say that some of us would be His witnesses. There are certain people who have a special gift of evangelism, but all of us are to witness. In *How to Give Away Your Faith*, Paul Little says, "Every Christian is a missionary. Any person who has been born into the family of God through faith and trust in Jesus Christ automatically receives the Lord's commission. Paul informed the Corinthians, 'We are ambassadors for Christ' (II Corinthians 5:20). To guard against misunderstanding or shirking of duty, he several times restates the fact that the ministry of reconciliation has been committed to us. God makes His appeal through you and me. We stand in Christ's stead beseeching men to be reconciled to God (II Corinthians 5:18-20). What a realization, when it finally grips us! Have you ever really considered this— that you are Jesus Christ to a lot of people? Nobody else. *You* are Jesus Christ to them." [15]

Acts 1:8 tells us that we *will be* witnesses. It is not something about which we have a choice. However, this does not mean that it comes naturally to us. We will be able to think of all kinds of reasons not to share our faith. (At least not right now!)

116

But each Christian must have an outreach if he is to grow and mature in faith. It is one of the ways in which spiritual health is maintained. Paul Little adds that when we have no personal outreach, "we . . . stifle ourselves spiritually, for we are denied the experience of seeing people genuinely born into the family of God. When we see no evidence of its redemptive power, the gospel begins to seem less real." This is undoubtedly the reason that Christianity seems to have so little effect on the lives of many professing Christians. Since they are not being used as instruments of the Holy Spirit to bring others to Christ, the whole thing takes on an air of unreality. Their religion seems removed from real life and of course eventually has very little to do with it. Their Christianity deteriorates to little more than an academic exercise.

Homemakers' Advantages in Witnessing

We homemakers have a distinct advantage in this area. Our ministry can often be broader and deeper than that of those in other professions because we can schedule the time for it, and we are able to use our homes for this purpose. However, we will have to make an effort, because we are not working among people all day long, as many of our husbands are.

Using Our Homes for Evangelism

There are many ways in which this can be done. We can drop in on our neighbors during the day and talk about Christ over a cup of coffee. Or we can invite our neighbors to our homes. This can even be done in groups. Several women in our area have begun speaking at informal evangelistic coffees and teas.* The hostess sends out written invitations to her non-Christian neigh-

---

* A manual, *Evangelistic Speaking and Entertaining*, is available from Campus Crusade headquarters or at Christian bookstores.

bors and friends to hear a speaker talk about "The Reality of Christianity in a Woman's World." After the guests have had coffee and cake, the hostess introduces the speaker. The speaker remains seated and very simply gives her personal testimony and then briefly explains the way of salvation, telling the women how they can commit their lives to Christ.

The response from the guests has been very favorable. Some women have understood, for the first time, what it really means to be a Christian, and have accepted Christ as Saviour. In some instances the result has been simply the building of a bridge for further communication. In fact, in every case that I have seen, a resulting benefit has been an easy, smooth breaking through the barriers of small talk and nonessentials that often separate us from real communication with others. One hostess told me that her relationships with all of her non-Christian friends are now much freer since she invited them to one of these coffees at her house. Her friends have a better understanding of what has happened in her life, and equally important, it is now out in the open. They no longer carefully avoid the subject.

This idea can also be used with couples. Husbands and wives are invited together in the evening and dessert and coffee are served before the speaker is introduced. Or rather "speakers." In this case a husband and wife speak as a team. Usually the husband gives his personal testimony, then the wife talks for a few minutes on how their being Christians affects their marriage and their relationship to their children. Then the husband takes over again and tells the group how they can commit their lives to Christ.

This format can be adapted for other mixed groups. My husband and I were asked to speak like this once for a rather large group of families at a dinner, and it worked out very well. In fact, the response from the teenagers present was as good as from the adults.

Leading Bible Studies

Having a Bible study with a friend or neighbor is another way of bringing the good news. When a person really gets into the Bible and sees what it is saying, the Holy Spirit begins to work. One need not be an experienced teacher in order to lead a Bible study. There are many excellent Bible study booklets and programs available. Some good ones are put out by the Navigators, Campus Crusade for Christ, and the World Home Bible League. I have used both Navigator and Campus Crusade materials and have found them to be very effective.

Most of these materials are set up in a way that you are not a teacher as such. You are simply leading the way as the two of you study the Bible together. Most use a question and answer method. If the person you are leading has a question which goes beyond the given material and which you are unable to answer, you can simply tell her that you do not know the answer to the question, but you will try to find it. Then you can bring the question to a qualified Bible teacher or pastor. As you become more experienced you will be able to answer most of the questions yourself. Seekers tend to ask many of the same questions, and you will soon become familiar with the different Scripture passages that answer them.

People Who Cross Our Paths

There are many opportunities to speak to people about Christ while we are going about our work, both in our homes and outside. For instance, there are the salespeople who come to our doors. After we have listened to them, we can politely ask them to listen to us. The man from whom we bought our encyclopedia became a Christian this way. He and his family then attended our church. There are people that we meet at school functions, or at the grocery store. If we belong to volunteer organizations we will become acquainted with women who need to hear the good news. Sometimes traveling will provide us with opportunities to speak of our faith. I have found trips by train, plane, or bus to be excellent for this. There is often a certain camaraderie between travelers which is conducive to conversation that goes beyond the exchange of pleasantries. These are moments that can be redeemed in the sense of Ephesians 5:16.

Usefulness of Personal Testimony

Our personal testimonies have a unique usefulness in evangelism. My husband is fond of saying, "No one can effectively argue with what has happened to you. He can try to disprove the Bible, he can argue against your theology, but he cannot argue with your experience with Christ." Alcoholics Anonymous understands the principle of the personal testimony and has used it to help thousands. At the meetings a man or woman will tell what his life was like before he came in contact with the organization, and what his life is like now. Other alcoholics can hear and see for themselves what has happened in this person's life and they realize it can happen to them too. In the same way Christians can convey the power of Christ through the use of testimonies.

Writing out our personal testimony is an important step in being prepared to share it with a non-Christian. At first this may seem superfluous and a bit silly. After all, we know what has happened to us. It is not some fiction we are inventing. Quite true. But in the tension and excitement of witnessing, we will not necessarily remember to stress the relevant parts of our experience if we have not organized our thoughts beforehand. A further danger is that without preparation what we tell may focus the attention on us instead of on Christ. I found that I never once effectively used any part of my testimony until I sat down and organized my thoughts and wrote it out, word for word. This does not mean that I have ever given it word for word, like an exercise in elocution. It comes out differently every time, since each person I speak to is different, and I relate to each one differently. But the important themes are always emphasized. Now that I have the outline firmly in my mind, I am freer to let the Spirit use me in speaking of my experience with the Lord.

Here are some guidelines that can be helpful in writing a personal testimony. Aim for about three minutes' length. Generally there will be three parts to a testimony: your life before, how you came to know Christ, and your life afterward. If you can pinpoint the exact time that you became a Christian, be sure to tell exactly how it happened so that your listeners will know how the same thing can happen to them. If, on the other hand, you grew up in a Christian home, always knowing that you belonged to Christ, your emphasis will be on the "after" part of your life.

If you have not had a dramatic conversion, do not think that your testimony is of less value. It is not necessary to have been a prostitute, a junkie, or a shoplifter in order to have your testimony be effective. Christians who have had these experiences before they met Christ can be powerfully used to reach others in similar predicaments. But most of the people you meet are ordinary folk with everyday problems and hangups. God will use your "ordinary" testimony to reach these people as they will be able to relate to you. In fact, often good, moral people do not respond to a dramatic testimony because they feel quite righteous by contrast.

It is best to avoid using Christian jargon. Words like "saved," "born again," "convicted," and "glorious" are good Biblical words which convey a wealth of meaning to Christians. But to a non-Christian they may be either meaningless or badly misunderstood. Keep the emphasis on Christ—on what He has done and is continuing to do in your life, not what you are doing.

As your testimony becomes a part of you, you will find yourself using it very naturally in your witnessing. And God will bless you.

Importance of Tools

In this area of your life, as in others, you will be the most effective when you have the tools and training which are suited for getting the job done in the best way possible. Evangelism training is extremely valuable. Methods are taught which have been developed over a length of time by many Christian leaders working together, praying together, and seeking the leading of the Holy Spirit. If your church sponsors a witnessing conference, or there is an institute for evangelism in your area, take the opportunity to attend and learn all you can.

D. J. Kennedy has developed an effective method to use in church calling programs which has been adopted by various churches. The Navigators use a method showing Christ as a bridge between God and man. There are various booklets put out by different denominations and organizations for use in evangelism. The Lutherans and Nazarenes each publish one, as does the Evangelism Department of the Christian Reformed Church. Theirs is called *The Good News for Modern Man.* Undoubtedly the most widely used of all is the *Four Spiritual Laws* put out by Campus Crusade for Christ. I have used both of these last two and have seen the Lord do mighty things through them. All of these booklets are available at Christian bookstores or by writing the organization. I am never without a supply. There is one in each of my purses, my Bible, my notebook, and the pockets of my various jackets. Using one of these tools is the best way I know to present the gospel in a form that is clear and scriptural, and yet complete enough so that the person understands how he can become a Christian. It also keeps the conversation centered on the person of Christ so that you do not get sidetracked.

Perhaps as important is the fact that it gives the person an opportunity to commit his life to Christ right at the moment. I have had many people tell me that they would have accepted Christ years earlier if only someone had made it clear to them just who Christ is and what is involved in becoming a Christian.

A few months ago a teen-aged boy I will call Steve visited our Sunday school. Our daughter noticed from the discussion that he did not have a clear understanding of how one becomes a Christian. After the class was over she shared the *Four Spiritual Laws* booklet with him and he prayed to commit his life to Christ. The next day he told his class in vacation Bible school that he had "come into the kingdom." He immediately began reading the Bible and attending church. In the next few weeks he read the first five books of the New Testament. He is excited about his new-found faith and is sharing it with others.

The thing about Steve that really made me stop and think again was his simple statement that he had wanted to become a Christian for a long time, but had never been able to find out how this could happen. He had attended church and discussed religion with his friends. But this was the first time that someone had showed him how he could become a Christian.

Jake is another example. He has been part of our church family for quite some time. He is thirty-eight years old, but being a casualty of a migrant worker's family, he never attended school long enough to learn to read and write. Perhaps this accounts for the fact that he can never remember exactly what the name of our church is. But he has said many times, "I know it's the right church, because it's the only one I ever found where they tell you how to become a Christian." Two of our young people shared one of the booklets with him while they were out calling one day. Later they called on his wife and she, too, became a Christian.

There are people all around us ready to respond to the gospel. Some, like Steve, know that they want to become Christians. Others, like Jake, do not. But they are waiting nonetheless. And using one of these tools allows you to be prepared to present the essentials of the gospel at all times.

Even if you have not had an opportunity to receive any training, you can effectively use one of these booklets. You simply read it through with the person. There are many ways that the booklet can be used in a conversation. Any time the talk is about goals, motivation, or beliefs, you can use it to show what yours are. If the conversation takes a "what is the world coming to?" turn, you have a perfect chance to explain with the booklet why you are not worried. As you ask for the Spirit's leading to make you alert to opportunities, you will find them.

These booklets can be used in group situations as well, such as the evangelistic coffees, or young people's groups.

Your tool can be useful when you have invited a friend to attend church with you. After church you can ask her what she thought of the sermon and if it made sense to her. You can then ask her if she, too, would like to become a Christian, and if she answers in the affirmative, you can take her through the booklet. You can do the same thing when you ask your friend her opinion of some Christian book you have given her to read.

Expect God to Use You

It is important to learn how to witness as well as possible; writing out your personal testimony is very helpful; it is important to use a tool; it is essential to be sure you are filled with the Spirit before attempting to share your faith; prayer is vital (talk to God about men before you talk to men about God). Then finally, expect results. Expect God to use you!

I am not talking about mere positive thinking. What

I am talking about is faith—taking God at His word. He has given us a job to do, and He has promised to see us through. He will give us whatever we need. Luke 11:13 says, "If you then, bad as you are, know how to give your children what is good for them, how much more will the heavenly Father give the Holy Spirit to those who ask him!" If we ask the Father He will give us a full measure of His Spirit, and we can expect Him to use us to bring others to himself.

Conclusion

Sharing our faith involves getting our priorities straight. It is easy for homemakers, like everyone else, to be so involved and busy with good things that we have no time for the best. Bill Bright often asks Christians, "What is the most important experience of your life?" They inevitably answer, "Knowing Christ as my Saviour." Then his second question is, "What is the most important thing you can do to help another person?" The answer is always the same, "Help him to know Christ." If we really believe that people are eternally lost without Christ, we will be serious about introducing others to our Saviour. This is the way that God, in His great wisdom, decided to use to spread His gospel. Romans 10:14 and 15 talks about the necessity of speaking out for Christ: "How (can anyone) hear without someone to spread the news?"

Verse 15 of the same chapter reminds us of something we are in danger of forgetting: "How welcome are the feet of the messengers of good news." Those whose hearts are prepared by the Holy Spirit will receive the gospel with joy. And joy then also wells up in the heart of the person who has brought the good news. There is probably no richer experience on earth than being the agent through which the Spirit works to bring another person to Himself. The deep inner happiness, excitement, and sense of fulfillment cannot be adequately described.

But in the final analysis, whether or not we are welcomed is not our problem. Neither need we worry about the response. We need only be obedient to the mandate given us. Some years ago I memorized a simple definition which is powerful in its wisdom. I pass it on to every evangelism class or group which I lead: "Success in witnessing is sharing your faith in the power of the Holy Spirit and leaving the results to God." We are not to worry about how many people respond. That is up to God. For after all is said and done, it is only God who can change the heart. That is only within His sovereign power. However, we can be sure He will bring people to himself in His own time. What *must* concern us is whether or not we are faithful.

CHAPTER 10

Making Disciples

Necessity for Discipling

Jesus told us in Matthew 28:19 and 20 to "go therefore and make disciples of all nations, . . . teaching them to observe all that I have commanded you . . ." (RSV). We have seen the importance of witnessing, of bringing the good news of salvation. The next step is teaching. After a person has taken the first step of faith, he must be helped to grow. His spiritual birth is only the beginning. To leave a new Christian at this point would be like leaving a small baby to fend for himself. Those people who have come to faith in Christ through us become our spiritual children. We are now responsible for their nurture. This is where discipling starts.

In this area we are probably closer to the New Testament situation today than at any time since the first century. The need for discipling is very apparent. We are finding more and more people—particularly young people—becoming Christians who know virtually nothing of "all that I have commanded you." They have no Biblical background at all. They have never attended church or Sunday school, or even opened a Bible.

Recently a young man (who subsequently became a Christian) told me matter-of-factly, "I'm glad to meet you. I've never met a minister or a minister's wife before." It is sad that we find ourselves in what some writers like to call the "post-Christian age." But it is a wonderful time in which to bring the gospel, and especially to make disciples. These new Christians who know little about Christ and their new life have no pre-conceived notions. There is nothing to unteach; there are no theological hang-ups. They are simply eager to learn everything they can from the Bible and from their teachers. It is a great experience to be able to relate the most basic Biblical truths and watch a person listening, wide-eyed as a child, delighted with the knowledge he is receiving.

New converts must be helped to grow. They need to begin to read the Bible, to pray, to get involved in church. Otherwise they will not progress, and their lives will go on very much as before. They will become spiritually retarded. Some new Christians seem to understand the need for Bible study, prayer, and worship, and will begin to do these things immediately, without anyone showing them the way. They seem to have been "born running." But these are the exceptions. Most need to be taken by the hand and carefully guided into the avenues of the Christian life.

Getting New Christians into the Church

A vitally important part of discipling new Christians is helping them to become a part of the church. As Samuel Shoemaker says in *With the Holy Spirit and with Fire*: "It looks as if the early Christians did not differentiate between getting into the stream and staying there through the fellowship of the Church. The personal decision to follow Christ was solidified by being made a member of His company, the Church. When a baby is born, it is normally born into a family." [16] The new Christian is born into God's family, the church, and needs to realize this.

Sometimes, however, this is not easy to accomplish. Many have been hurt by the church. They have gotten the impression that the church was only after their money, that they were being used instead of helped, or that they were shunned because they were not socially acceptable. Sometimes the people themselves were at fault, but in other instances the church *has* been insensitive to people's needs, has pursued its own prestige and welfare instead of fulfilling its real purpose. Others look at the church and see that its membership includes those who are living like non-Christians and want nothing to do with it.

The way to deal with these problems is to divert attention from the people in the church and focus on Christ. These new Christians need to see that although the church may contain people whose lives are inconsistent with true Christian character, God has chosen to work through the church, and Christians are commanded to identify with it. But we must be patient as we teach and encourage these tender young converts. The more they see Christ in us and the more they want to imitate us in our Christian life, the easier it will be to bring them to church with us and help them to become involved. And *bringing them with us* is crucial. We must recognize that for people to enter a new gathering all by themselves is very difficult, sometimes frightening. Our telling them how welcome they are makes little difference. For the first few times we must arrange to stop at their house, pick them up, and bring them with us.

Do Not Expect Instant Maturity

This business of discipling takes time. Although we often see a person experience a dramatic conversion which takes place in a moment, his Christian walk will go on for the rest of his life. This process of becoming holy—more Christlike and mature—is a life-long process. Once a person becomes a Christian his direction is changed, his deepest desires are different. But he may not have instant mastery over all the temptations in his life. In fact, he probably will not recognize some of them as temptations at first. In time the Spirit will point out these areas in his life to him, and he will begin to deal with them. We who are older in the faith must not expect a new Christian to be at the same point spiritually that we are, when it took us years to get there.

A teenager of my acquaintance who has been a Christian for a year of stormy ups and downs says that at first he would realize he had sinned after it had happened, then gradually he began to be aware of sins while he was committing them, and now he finally recognized the temptation beforehand, in time to do something about it. He still has by no means won the battle against his old style of life. His friends put tremendous pressures on him, and he has not yet been able to make a break with them. Peer pressures can be a powerful tool of the devil, particularly with young people, but often with adults as well.

As a Christian community it is important for us to realize that none of us is without sin, either, but often our sins are of the more secret or "acceptable" variety. Perhaps we gossip, worry, covet, become angry, lust, or cheat on our income tax. Many of these sins are not so obvious, and others we simply accept in ourselves and each other. A new Christian's sins, on the other hand, are often much more clear to us. We are not used to them, and so they stand out in bold relief against our style of life. If we are aware of this, we can avoid the trap of Phariseeism. We are called to love people unconditionally, even while they are stumbling and falling as they learn to walk.

Sometimes new Christians will even become rebellious against God and against His people, the church. They may settle back into their old sinful habits and then become defensive. Or they may keep seeing their old friends who begin dragging them down again. Or they may neglect to confess their sins as they become aware of them. Their relationship with God is short-circuited, and they become miserable. Then they become irritated when other Christians, by their very lives, show them up. So they begin to lash out at other Christians, and at the church. A further complication is that many people today have been brought up to be very suspicious of authority. They instinctively rebel against *any* kind of authority, and that includes the church.

The only way to treat new Christians who are "out of it" spiritually is in love. We must keep on loving them, and keep on showing them that we do, no matter how bad their behavior is. We must say, in effect, "God isn't going to give up on you and I'm not either. No matter how bad you may act, I'll be here when you need me."

Recently a young woman who has been a Christian for about a year and a half told me that she never would have made it if we in the church had not kept on loving her, even when she seemed to be rejecting us. Even though it seemed she wanted nothing more to do with us, we never gave up on her. We knew that she was a child of God and that she needed us.

Qualifications for Discipling

But how does one, specifically a homemaker who is not a trained teacher, go about this business of making disciples?

All of us can teach someone. In the previous chapter we talked about different Bible study courses and booklets that are available. Using one of them is probably the simplest and most effective way of leading your student in the study of God's Word. The only qualification necessary is that you be a disciple of Christ yourself.

A disciple is a follower. He is a learner; he must have an open, teachable spirit. Paul was a master discipler. He had the confidence to say in Philippians 3:17, "Keep on imitating me, brothers, all of you. We have set the right example for you" (TEV). And yet he says in verses 12 and 13 that he has not yet become all that Christ wants him to be: "I do not claim that I have already succeeded in this, or have already become perfect. I keep going on to try to possess it, for Christ Jesus has already possessed me. Of course, brothers, I really do not think that I have already reached it; the one thing I do, however, is to forget what is behind me and do my best to reach what is ahead." He was continually learning, all of his life.

So perfect knowledge or maturity is not a requirement for being a disciple or a maker of disciples. It is the openness to Christ which is important. We must be letting Christ change us. We must be growing, and growth means change. This is often difficult for us to face—sometimes even painful. We do not like to admit that things in our lives need changing. And then when, in spite of ourselves, we *have* changed, we often try to deny it if someone mentions it. We are comfortable with ourselves the way we are. But Christ demands that we be constantly growing and changing. Romans 12:2 reads, "Let your minds be remade and your whole nature thus transformed."

A disciple is also disciplined. (The two words come from the same root.) This means that we must organize our lives and then do what we know must be done. A master discipler of our day says, "Plan your work and then work your plan." We must pull up the loose ends of our lives, ignore the many distractions, and get on with our business.

A part of being disciplined is getting our priorities in order. We must decide which things are of vital importance and thus should take the largest share of our time, which things should have only a small part of our time, and which things are really not worth our time at all. This may mean giving up some things which are dear to us or which we enjoy very much. Perhaps God will show us that we must not take the time to watch television, or go on frequent shopping expeditions. Each woman will be called to order her life somewhat differently. However, getting our priorities straight means not letting anything get in the way of our vocation as Christians, which is to follow Christ: to honestly look at what *He* wants us to do and then do it.

Jesus put the matter quite bluntly to His would-be followers while He was on earth. Luke 9:55-62 tells of three men who wanted to follow Him. They wanted to be His disciples. But each had something else in his life to which he gave priority. Jesus will never accept second place. His final comment in verse 62 was unequivocal: "No one who sets his hand to the plough and then keeps looking back is fit for the kingdom of God."

Examples Set for Us

We can learn a lot of the how-to of discipling from looking at how Jesus taught His disciples. He spent a great deal of time alone with the twelve, pouring himself into them. He answered their questions, pointed them to the Scriptures and to His Father's will. He taught them how to pray and how to witness. He was available whenever they had a problem. And then He narrowed His teaching down still further in singling out Peter, James, and John for special discipling.

Paul also preached to and taught many people but singled out a few, such as Timothy and Titus.

Teaching Prayer

Teaching our students to pray is an important part of discipling. Some new Christians immediately begin talking to God quite naturally and freely, but most need help in this area. Some have a mistaken notion that there is a special language they need to learn for prayer. (Unfortunately, they have heard prayers using stilted, formal language and stereotyped phrases; they think they must do the same.) Others are terrified at the thought of praying aloud. We need to explain to them and show them that there is nothing complicated or scary about prayer—that it is simply talking to God.

Teaching the different aspects of prayer is helpful. An often-used memory device is the word ACTS, each letter of which represents a part of prayer: adoration—simply praising God for who and what He is; confession—confessing our sins and telling God we are sorry and need forgiveness; thanksgiving—thanking Him for all He has done and is doing for us; and supplication—bringing our requests to God.

Also, prayer must be specific. We must confess specific sins (otherwise it is hard to be sorry), we must thank God for specific blessings, and we must make specific requests. Happily, most new Christians tend to be very open and forthright with God. They have never learned to pray in vague generalities for "all those who are in need of help," etc. In fact, they are often so specific that it may be startling for us at first. We need only watch that we do not impose our bad patterns of prayer on them. Perhaps we could afford to catch a bit of their spontaneity instead.

We will explain these different aspects of prayer to our students, but they will learn only as they actually being to pray. And this means praying aloud. If they are hesitant, we can patiently and lovingly encourage them and if necessary gently nudge them to get started. Once they have broken through, it will not take long until they are praying quite naturally and easily.

We mentioned earlier that unconfessed sins can stand in the way of a new Christian's growth. This point is worth elaborating. It is important for new Christians to learn that they must confess their sins as soon as they become aware of them. Unconfessed sins separate us from God. Psalm 66:18 tells us that if we are harboring sin in our hearts, He will not hear us. Our prayers will not get through to God and we will not be able to commune with Him. As soon as we become Christians our sins are covered by the blood of Christ, of course. But sins of which we are aware but which we have not confessed can and will stand in the way of our fellowship with God. For a new Christian this can be disastrous.

Multiplication the Aim

Paul gives us some excellent guidelines in the classic verse on discipling: "You heard my teaching in the presence of many witnesses; put that teaching into the charge of men you can trust, such men as will be competent to teach others" (II Tim. 2:2). In other words, we must be trying to reproduce ourselves in people who will also reproduce. So our aim is to bring our students to the point where they will also be sharing their faith and teaching others.

This will take concentrated effort. Besides your regular Bible study and prayer time together, you will want to take your student with you as you share your faith with others. If you are teaching a Sunday school class or women's group, let her observe. She can be your Timothy. As she watches you as you minister, she will soon come to realize that she can begin to do some of the same things. Then as she does begin to witness and teach, you will be available to help her over the rough spots. When she gets to this point, you can suggest that she begin to look and pray for someone that *she* can be discipling.

Finding God's Will

During your Bible study time, you will be explaining how your student can relate her faith to her life. She will begin to see changes which must be made, decisions that will be different from before. The same principle that applies to child-raising is applicable here: pointing to God's will.

Finding God's will is not always easy. There are certain guidelines that can help us. First and foremost, of course, is the authority of Scripture. This takes precedence over all the other guidelines. On some questions about which we must make decisions the Bible is very clear. In that case we need no further help.

The second guideline is our reason, used according to Biblical principles. God has given us intelligence to use. When faced with a decision, we are not to put our minds out of gear and blindly grope for an answer. We must carefully think the decision through, considering the probable consequences of the different alternatives. For example, in disciplining our children we must consider what the results of a certain method are likely to be.

We are also to consider the particular circumstances in which we find ourselves. Our circumstances are part of God's providence, of His continual care over us. For instance, God has placed us among certain people for a reason. He has also given us education or particular gifts for a reason. These are circumstances which must be considered when making certain decisions.

In addition, there is the leading of the Holy Spirit in our hearts. I quickly add a word of caution here, because this guideline is the most difficult to follow correctly and is often badly misused by Christians. It is important to use this guideline *only in connection with the other three.* Otherwise we are in danger of listening to the wrong spirit. The Holy Spirit never tells us to do anything that is contrary to the Scripture or contrary to that reason which is based on the Word of God. For instance, after sleeping late and missing church while her non-Christian friend was dressed and waiting to attend with her, a woman told me that this had been God's will. This was not a responsible seeking of God's will. She was merely trying to excuse herself. Others follow their own desires and whims and think that they are following the direction of the Holy Spirit.

What we feel in our hearts is not always the Holy Spirit's desire. Our own wishes and desires are in our hearts as well. Galatians 5:17 reads, "For we naturally love to do evil things that are just the opposite from the things that the Holy Spirit tells us to do; and the good things we want to do when the Spirit has his way with us are just the opposite of our natural desires. These two forces within us are constantly fighting each other to win control over us, and our wishes are never free from their pressures" (Living Bible). So when something within us is telling us to do a certain thing, we must carefully test to see what spirit it is.

Finally, the advice of mature Christian counselors can be helpful. Sometimes we are so close to our problems that we cannot see them in perspective. A pastor, parents, or a Christian teacher can serve as counselors. But we must be sure that these people are using these guidelines for finding God's will. Otherwise they may be swayed by their own emotions or prejudices.

When we teach young Christians to look for what God wants in each situation, they will be maturing in attitudes and actions as they grow in knowledge.

Older Christians Need Discipling Too

We will be discipling those people that we have led to Christ, of course. But sometimes there are others that God puts in our path who need us. There are many Christians who have never known what it is to live a full-orbed, vibrant Christian life. No one ever taught them that faith is to relate to the whole of life, that everything must be seen in the light of God's will for their lives. When they see what the Christian life is really all about,

137

many of them are very eager to be discipled. As you are witnessing you will find many people like this. When they meet a Christian who is excited about Jesus and telling others about Him, they want to find out how they, too, can have this abundant life. They will see that you have a quality of life that they do not have, and they will want to learn from you.

Our Children as Disciples

Recently a group of us were discussing the difference between a Christian family and a non-Christian family. A teen-aged boy who knows my children turned to me and said, "It must be easy for you to be a parent, because you have Christian kids." For a moment I was at a loss for an answer. I had never heard that bit of logic before. This young man has been a Christian only a short time, and of course there are gaps in his knowledge of the faith. He evidently has the idea that my children were automatically Christian at birth, in the same way that they were born blonde and blue-eyed. However, it is not that simple. We have noted that we must take responsibility for our children's Christian nurture in order to claim them for Christ.

They will not automatically become *disciples* just because we are. We have all heard of godly men and women whose children have gone astray. We must take every opportunity to teach them, to share our faith-in-action with them. Timothy was carefully taught, from early childhood on, by his godly mother and grandmother. This is very likely the reason that Paul could depend on him at such a young age for so much in the work of spreading the gospel.

The Navigators often send a new Christian to live for a time with a person who is older in the faith so that the young Christian can learn firsthand what the life in Christ is all about. This can be a growing experience for both people involved. The disciple learns much, both by watching and by continually sharing thoughts and insights with his teacher. The teacher, at the same time, is constantly aware of his responsibility to show Christ in his daily life. He must be always on his mettle spiritually. He knows that if he would begin to live a defeated spiritual life, for example, it would have a disastrous effect on the young Christian in his charge. This helps the teacher to stand a little taller, spiritually.

All of us who have children are in very much the same position as this Navigator. Our children are younger in faith as well as years, and they are watching us to see what the Christian life really is. What a marvelous opportunity for discipling! We can reproduce ourselves spiritually in our children so that what Paul said of the Corinthians can be said of them, "They can see that you are a letter from Christ written by us. It is not a letter written with pen and ink, but by the Spirit of the living God; . . . carved . . . in human hearts" (II Cor. 3:3, Living Bible).

There are several ways in which our children can be our Timothys. As soon as they are old enough to read the Bible, we can explain the importance of personal devotions to them, and help them to begin having their own quiet time. This will take some attention from us. Habits like this are not established overnight. Naturally it is easier to accomplish when they have been aware that *we* have a time set aside for our own devotions.

Long before they are able to read the Bible, we can be teaching our children to pray. (Not to "say prayers," but to really talk to God.) We can teach them to pray aloud and to lead others in prayer. Conversational or sentence prayers are often a good way to begin praying in front of others. Children who are used to joining in conversational prayers at home will have no trouble praying with others later on.

From the time they are quite small, they can be involved in our ministry as prayer partners. As we share our faith with others and begin to instruct them, we can be telling our children about it. If we are excited about what we are doing, if we communicate by our enthusiasm how important this is to us, our children will catch the vision. We can be explaining to them what we are doing and how we are going about it. Then by the time they are teenagers our children can also be sharing their faith and beginning to teach others.

There are few satisfactions for a parent equal to seeing one's young son or daughter bringing others to Christ and then leading them in the study of God's Word and the Christian life. Discipling our children in this way requires time and effort from us. But in return we find a measure of true fulfillment which is only experienced by one who is in the center of God's will.

Modern Translations of the Bible a Blessing

It is important for a child or a new Christian who is beginning to read the Bible to have a Bible that he *can* read. Most of us who have grown up in the church love the King James Version. It is poetic; it falls beautifully on our ears. Besides, we have memorized large portions of it, and these passages just do not seem the same in another translation. I often find myself going back to check on certain familiar passages and saying, "Ah, yes, *that's* the way it goes." But we must face the fact that for the overwhelming majority of people today the King James Version is virtually unreadable.

Recently in my Sunday school class I asked a fifth-grader to read a passage. For two verses he tried valiantly to cope with the archaic language in his King James Bible. When he had finished he had no idea what he had read. I had to "translate" four of the important words for the class.

The limitations of the Authorized Version were brought home to me in a striking fashion a few months ago. In our Wednesday night Bible study group, we were studying different books of the Bible by writing our own paraphrases. I decided not to read any of the published paraphrases or newer translations, so that my writing would be my own. Since I cannot read the ancient languages, I was limited to the King James Version. In the course of our study I was shocked and somewhat embarrassed to discover that there were several verses that I could not paraphrase without help because, try as I might, I simply could not get the meaning from the King James Bible. I discovered that I had read many of those passages for years without really understanding them. The point is that if we want the Bible to be read and understood, we must see to it that people have it in a form they can understand.

We have been blessed in the last few years with a great many new readable translations. Two that are extensively used are the *Living New Testament* (also under other titles, such as *Reach Out* and *The Greatest Is Love*) and *Today's English Version* or *Good News for Modern Man*. Both of these are easy to understand, although the *Good News* uses a more limited vocabulary. It can be read and understood by quite young children. *The Living New Testament* is a paraphrase, of course, and as such has limitations. Although in many ways I consider it to be the most powerful of all (hard truths which can somehow be ignored in some of the other versions seem to jump right up and hit me in the *Living Bible*), it is the work of one man and is not an exact translation. The writer's theological bent comes through strongly in certain passages. It should be used alongside one of the other versions. But for those who are just beginning to read the Bible, the *Living Bible* is extremely useful. On its pages Biblical truths make the transition from religious jargon to exciting reality.

So making disciples requires that we ourselves be spiritually on target. We must be following Christ in a way that is worthy of being imitated. And then we must stick close to our students, showing them how their faith relates to all areas of their lives, how they can make their decisions in the light of God's will. This involves leading them in Bible study and prayer, helping them to get involved in church, and teaching them how to share their faith and teach others, It also means being available for counsel when problems come up or temptations hit.

This may sound like a tall order. It is. It is for those willing to turn the world upside-down. It is not for those lacking in spiritual courage. But then, as C. S. Lewis points out, where there is no courage, the other virtues are seldom of much use. So let us get on with the task, large as it is, taking heart from the knowledge that Christ never commands us to do something that He does not give us the power to do. At the same time that He gives us the command in Matthew 28:19 and 20 to teach and make disciples, He promises that while we are doing this, ". . . be assured, I am with you always, to the end of time."

CHAPTER 11

Recreation

Necessity for Recreation

According to Webster the word "recreation" means "creating anew, restoring, refreshing: refreshment of strength and spirits after toil." Since all of life belongs to God, our recreation is also part of our total service. Sometimes our leisure can have an additional purpose beyond simply relaxation, but this does not mean that it is any less recreation.

All other workers and professional people have certain days and hours when they are not working, when they are off-duty. Since there are no nicely drawn limits to our job as homemakers, there may be a tendency for us to work too long and hard. Because some of us are on call twenty-four hours a day, seven days a week, we need to schedule certain blocks of time to recreate. We need not feel guilty about this. It is not only allowable, it is necessary for our physical, emotional, and mental well-being.

Resting

Sometimes the best way to refresh a weary mind and body is the obvious way: sleep. I am a great advocate of afternoon naps. I believe every pregnant or nursing mother should do her best to get a daily nap, and no hard-working homemaker should be apologetic about resting for a short time in the afternoon. If you can train yourself to actually sleep for a half hour or so, great! If not, just relaxing can do wonders. Our children all took naps until they started kindergarten—partly because *they* needed it, partly because *I* did.

Exercise

Although to the unaccustomed it may sound like more work, exercise, when properly done, can be very refreshing. A good brisk walk (pushing oneself to stride as fast as possible), jog, or swim can be the best possible tonic for fatigue. In fact, a daily program of moderate exercise can often prevent tiredness and fatigue. An exercise such as jogging (as opposed to calisthenics or spot-reducing exercises) gets the circulation going at a good rate, moderately raises the blood sugar level, and generally allows the body to function more efficiently. As the heart rate increases, the blood works more efficiently to carry the chemicals in the body to the liver where they are broken down and detoxified. The movement of muscles produces a substance in the body which acts as a natural tranquilizer. This is why exercise is so helpful for persons who are depressed or who just have a touch of the doldrums.

I have never been the athletic type. And since I have never had a tendency to put on weight, I have never bothered to exercise either. But recently I began jogging and striding. I find it very exhilarating, and if I miss a couple of days I can often tell the difference in my sense of well-being.

Hobbies

Any number of hobbies can provide a much-needed diversion, from engaging in sports, to playing a musical instrument, singing in a group, or working at a favorite craft project. Some things, such as sewing or gardening, can be hobbies for one woman and simply more work for another. Each woman must choose the activity which relaxes and refreshes her.

Vacations

Vacations and trips are good ways of getting away from one's job. And they can provide a necessary change of pace. The trouble is, for a homemaker a vacation can be more of the same work in a different setting. Often she is still making meals, cleaning the cabin or rooms, and taking care of the children. Even if she does not have to cook, the children are usually her responsibility. (As every mother knows, Father can be theoretically in charge, but as soon as any little thing comes up they run to Mother anyway.) If it can possibly be arranged, a week's vacation with only her husband can be a wonderful holiday for a wife and mother. If a whole week is impossible, even a day or two can work wonders.

Letter Writing

Writing to family and friends can be a wonderful creative outlet. Ideas and experiences shared with a friend are enjoyed twice. And there is the added enjoyment of knowing that your letter will bring pleasure to the recipient.

Reading

One of the fringe benefits of homemaking that means the most to me is having time to read and study. I am able to take the time to read books that are helping to shape our culture today as well as those that are part of our literary and religious heritage.

This reading is relaxation; it is a part of our leisure. And yet it plays an important part in equipping us to do our job in the best way possible. For instance, there are many books that can help us in raising our children, giving us specific directions and advice. Reading good magazines and newspapers helps us to keep up with current events. This is essential for anyone who wants to be involved in the community in a meaningful way. It is pretty difficult to help when you are not aware of what the needs are. To be involved you must be informed.

In addition there is a whole wealth of literature which simply helps to make us bigger persons. Good books expand our horizons and broaden our imaginations. They give pleasure, delight, and spiritual enrichment. This is real recreation: refreshing our minds and spirits so that we are renewed. And the more we grow as persons, the more we can inspire and challenge our children and those whom we are discipling and counseling to share our vision.

Here are a few of the novels I have especially enjoyed:

Oliver Twist and *David Copperfield*, both by Charles Dickens. These two novels give insights into the problems of England in that day. Dickens has the ability to touch the reader's deepest emotions—you will laugh and cry all the way through these books.

The Scarlet Letter by Nathaniel Hawthorne. A heart-rending tale of a woman discovered to be an adulteress and her lover, who tries to hide his guilt. The problem of relating the Puritan ethic to life.

Huckleberry Finn and *Tom Sawyer* by Mark Twain. Good, sunny humor giving a picture of America a century ago.

The Great Gatsby by F. Scott Fitzgerald. This is probably the best novel portraying life in the "roaring twenties."

The Grapes of Wrath by John Steinbeck. A novel about the plight of the Okies during the depression which gripped the conscience of the country. This book has been called the latter-day *Uncle Tom's Cabin*.

The Old Man and the Sea by Ernest Hemingway. A picture of the futility of life as Hemingway saw it.

The Hobbit and *The Lord of the Rings* (a trilogy) by J.R.R. Tolkien. These should not be missed. The author, a Christian, creates for us the fantasy world of Middle Earth, inhabited by the amiable hobbits and other creatures of darker purposes. In spinning his masterful tale of suspense, he deals with the eternal theme of good versus evil. Once you start these volumes you will read them long into the night.

Dr. Zhivago by Boris Pasternak. The struggles of the people during the Russian revolution.

The Blood of the Lamb by Peter DeVries. A sensitive father watches the agonizing death of a child from leukemia.

Lord of the Flies by William Golding. The author shows, very dramatically, the sinful nature of man. A group of young boys are shipwrecked on a lush island—a veritable Paradise. At first everything looks rosy. The older boys take care of the younger ones, there is plenty of food, etc. By the end of the book they have committed all manner of heinous crimes, including murder, and are in danger of exterminating each other.

And some poetry:

T. S. Eliot, *The Complete Poems and Plays*, particularly "Choruses from 'The Rock'" and *The Cocktail Party*. A perceptive treatment of the decadence of modern times.

W. H. Auden, "For the Time Being." Insights into Biblical thought. The reader will recognize the author as a kindred spirit.

Edna St. Vincent Millay, *Second April* and *The Buck in the Snow*.

The following is an additional list of recommended books and commentary prepared for me by Dr. John Timmerman and Dr. Stanley Wiersma, both professors of English at Calvin College:

Alan Paton, *Too Late the Phalarope* and *Cry the Beloved Country*. Here the race problem is laid out in a South African situation, all the more valuable because it is so far removed from us, and the moral issues are so clear. Seeing what the issues are—stark and simple—in Paton's novels makes it easier to see them in our own neighborhood again.

James Baldwin, *Go Tell It on the Mountain*. The black problem from a black teenager's point of view. An excellent look at black religion in America. The whole problem of a white Jesus comes up, especially when you read the novel against the more strictly autobiographical *The Fire Next Time*. The boy tells himself he is never going to grovel in front of the altar, giving his heart to Jesus, but that is just what he ends up doing. And having knuckled under to the white Jesus, he will knuckle under to the whole system: Uncle Tom shuffling, lazy slave act, etc.

C. S. Lewis, *That Hideous Strength, Perelandra, Out of the Silent Planet*—The Space Trilogy, as it is sometimes called. The over-all problem is the share that the devil has in science and technology. C. S. Lewis has an uncanny way of smelling the touch of the devil in us all, especially smelling out how we ourselves have sold out our Christian principles to the scientific method, without realizing it.

Muriel Spark, *Memento Mori*. The problem of old age. Rest homes are never so purely restful as the name would imply. A "sociologist" runs a little experiment, calling up people on the phone, old people, all of them, and saying simply, without identifying himself: "Remember, you must die." Each reacts quite differently. Death gives life a new focus.

Flannery O'Connor, *The Complete Stories*. She writes

about grotesques who find the kingdom of God. She is against the sophisticated and worldly-wise. The foolish and ugly people of the world have an automatic "in" with the gospel.

Christopher Fry, Two plays: *A Phoenix Too Frequent* and *Venus Observed*, dealing with the problems of grief, and women's roles in the world, respectively.

Phyllis McGinley, *Times Three*, a series of poems on the saints in which they come on so funny and human.

Lawrence Dorr, *A Slow, Soft River*. The problems of being a saint in wartime, written by a Hungarian refugee.

Additional novels:

Asch, S., *Mary*

Bennett, A., *The Old Wives' Tale*

Brick, John, *The Rifleman*

Buck, Pearl, *The New Year*

Cather, W., *My Antonia, Shadows on the Rock, Sapphira and the Slave Girl*

Chase, M. E., *The Lovely Ambition, Windswept*

Clark, W., *The Ox-Bow Incident*

Conrad, J., *Victory*

deWohl, *The Spear*

Coblentz, *The Bells of Leyden Sing*

Douglas, *The Robe*

Edmonds, *Drums Along the Mohawk*

Ellis, *The Bounty Lands, Jonathan Blair, Bounty Lands Lawyer*

Garth, *Fire on the Wind*

Glasgow, E., *This Barren Ground*

Holt, V., *Mistress of Melynn*

James, H., *The Turn of the Screw*

Lancaster, B., *The Secret Road*

Lofts, N., *Katherine of Aragon*

MacInnes, H., *North from Rome*

Powers, J. F., *Morte D'urban*

Parker, *The Seats of the Mighty*

Reade, *The Cloister and the Hearth*
Roberts, K., *Oliver Wiswell*
Roolvaag, *Giants in the Earth*
Stewart, M., *The Crystal Cave*
Trollop, A., *Barchester Towers*
Webb, *Precious Bane*
Webb, M., *The Advocate*
Walker, M., *Jubilee*
Werfel, F., *Hearken Unto the Voice*
Wharton, E., *The Age of Innocence*
Wilder, T., *The Bridge of San Luis Rey*
Wibberley, L., *The Hands of Cormac Joyce*
Zara, *Blessed Is the Man*

CHAPTER 12

Moonlighting

Pressures to Leave the Home

Only a generation ago the wife and mother with an outside job was the rare exception. Certainly we were not more affluent then. Just the opposite. In American families the principal bread-winner's income, even adjusted to take inflation into account, has risen considerably over the past generation. But at that time community pressure on women to remain at home was strong. This was so, particularly among certain Christian groups.

However, almost overnight this has changed. Women have become a "cause," perhaps the most popular one around. As people have rallied to the aid of blacks, the poverty-stricken, and the underprivileged, they are now fighting for the rights of women. And the "right" that seems to be fought for the most is the right to leave our homes for some other career, which, they tell us, will be vastly more satisfying and fulfilling.

We are bombarded daily with advertising that insists

we buy more and more. A second paycheck begins to look very alluring. Having been told persistently in the last few years that housework and child care are repetitious and boring, even the most hardy of us become vulnerable to feelings of discontent. We begin to feel vaguely unfulfilled and unchallenged. Those of us with college degrees or specialized training are probably hit the hardest. The world out there *needs* us, we are told; our special abilities must not be allowed to deteriorate. If we have children, it is the business of society to see to it that they are cared for, according to this reasoning. We may even begin to feel *guilty* about staying home.

Unless we think about our role as wives and mothers by asking what God's will is in this matter, we will find ourselves being sucked into this broad stream of society. Perhaps we will find ourselves rushing in a direction we ought not be going. Our calling, according to Romans 12:2, is not to conform to society, but to be transformed.

Family Set Up by God

God has set up the family as the basic unit of society. From the beginning He has worked out His redemptive plan through the family. The denomination to which I belong even counts its membership by families, which I believe, is proper. When we are carrying out our responsibilities as Christian parents the way God expects us to, the entire family belongs to Him and to His church.

Family Life Weakened When Mother Leaves

If we wives and mothers start dividing our commitment and energy between our families and outside careers, family life will be weakened. Even some women in the women's lib movement are becoming alarmed about the direction family life is taking. In the August, 1972 issue of *McCall's*, Dr. Mary Rowe is quoted as saying that homemaking is the one profession that is "basic to a healthy society." [17] She is concerned that often a homemaker is not considered by society to be doing valuable, productive work. She is looking for ways to give house-wives the recognition they deserve so that society will not completely disintegrate. Although she herself has left her home for another job, she seems to realize that if everyone did, we would have chaos.

The Effect on Husbands

Husbands seldom really want their wives to have out-side jobs. Yet not many men will actually insist that their wives stay home. The social climate today is such that this would require the kind of courage that few men possess. Today it is almost easier to be against mother-hood than to keep a woman from "fulfilling" herself out-side of the home. But it becomes clear in conversations with husbands that they really want their wives to be full-time homemakers.

Even those people who strongly advocate women leaving the home for outside jobs admit that husbands seldom like it. In the February, 1969 *McCall's*, Sylvia Hartman challenges women to get out of the house. Talk-ing about husbands she writes, "It seems pretty clear that no man is really crazy about the idea of his wife's working. . . . A wife who works . . . will at times be tired and preoccupied—and her husband will suffer as a re-sult. . . . If she has a deadline, he may have to get his own supper that night." Yet she goes on to say that this has no bearing on the subject because of women's rights. Husbands have been made to feel guilty about wanting their wives home, so very often they give in. And Chris-tians are giving in right along with everyone else. How-ever, if we are taking our calling as wives in Christ seri-ously, we will respect our husbands' real wishes. We will look at how we can best serve them, not how we can best be served.

Often a woman must hold an outside job to help her husband through school or because of a compelling emergency. But when a woman works outside the home simply to supplement her husband's income, the effect on her husband can be very serious. His ability to care for his family has been challenged—as a provider he has been weighed in the balance and found lacking. Very likely he and his wife discussed the matter together and decided that her taking an outside job was the sensible answer. Perhaps he even suggested this as a solution to their money problems. No matter. He still has to face the fact that his efforts at making a living for the family have not been successful. This is a serious blow to a husband's ego, whether he admits it or not. He begins to have little nagging doubts about his success as a husband and father, and as a man.

I remember a young man saying exactly that. For several years he had held a good position. Then he and his wife decided to move to California in search of still better opportunities. At first he had to take a job which did not pay very well. Soon the employer had to let some of his men go. Since this young man was the last one hired, he was the first to go. He found another stop-gap job, and the pattern repeated itself. Soon his record began to look bad. He had had too many jobs in too short a time. Prospective employers were hesitant to hire him. He began to lose faith in himself.

Since he was working at jobs which did not pay as much as he would have liked, his wife decided that she should get an outside job so that the family would have financial security. Then she began to lose faith in him as a provider. She also began to feel financially independent.

Sometime later while we were visiting together, the husband stated quite matter-of-factly that he found it hard to really feel like a man while his wife was out working because she felt she had to. The marriage subsequently became very shaky and was nearly broken. When circumstances forced this wife to become a full-time home-

154

maker again, their marriage stabilized.

The wife who is serious in her concern for her husband's welfare will give up luxuries, budget carefully, and learn to live on her husband's income. I am convinced that a woman who is committed to living on her husband's income can do it. Although I have met some extravagant husbands as well as wives, in most cases the wife is the one who insists on a higher standard of living. Perhaps we women have a better appreciation for nice things. A more likely explanation is that we spend more of our time working with the material trappings of our lives. We are responsible for the care of the furnishings of our homes; we must buy or sew the family's clothes, and prepare the family's food. So the temptation is always in front of us to covet nicer furniture, finer clothes, and shinier appliances.

If the carpet is becoming worn, or the kitchen is not color-coordinated, most husbands will not be particularly concerned. Many do not even notice such things. Some husbands (mine included) must be encouraged, if not pushed, into a store to purchase new clothes for themselves. On the other hand, we must look rather hard to find a wife who will not immediately act on her husband's suggestion to buy a new outfit.

So when it seems as if a wife must get an outside job so the family can manage, she should ask herself whether the family really needs additional income, or whether she is projecting her own desires onto her family. It is possible that her husband and children would be just as happy without that new stove, sofa, or additional clothes. Ostensibly she may be taking an outside job to get money for such legitimate things as orthodontia or the children's education. However, these things can usually be managed on the husband's income when a wife is willing to take an honest look at what the family's real needs are and to manage accordingly.

The Effect on Children

Children miss out on much that they need when a woman is committed to another job. Advocates of other careers for mothers are fond of saying, "It's not the *quantity* of time you spend with a child that's important, but the *quality* of that time." This sounds very nice, but it is misleading on two counts. First of all, how can a mother give her child quality time after she has given the best hours of her day to another job? When she comes home she is tired and probably rushed as well, as she hurriedly fixes dinner and does whatever chores are necessary to prepare for work the next day. Very likely she is in no mood to answer her child's questions or spend time reading to him. What is left of her day is simply not quality time. Her own pressing need to relax and unwind from the pressures of her day is likely to take precedence over everything else.

The second thing wrong with this reasoning is that what makes time with a child quality time is often determined by the child or by circumstances beyond the mother's control. When the school nurse calls to say my child is sick and I rush to school to get her, I am spending quality time with her. When my pre-schooler rushes in to get me to look at a splendid ant colony she has discovered in the field, that is quality time. When one of them needs comforting and I am there, that is quality time. There is no way that these experiences can be saved up to be delivered at the mother's convenience.

Most experts in child care still believe that it is best for children, particularly young children, to have their mother around most of the time. Louise Bates Ames talks about this in an article in the April, 1972 *Family Circle* entitled "Should Mothers Work?" She is arguing for other careers for mothers, yet she admits: "Most of those concerned with the welfare of children do still feel that the infant and pre-schooler does best if he can spend those early, tender years in the rather constant presence

156

of his mother. There is much that needs to be worked through as he separates himself emotionally from that person of whom he was once a physical part. It can best be accomplished if his mother is right there with him for much of the time." [18]

In the October, 1972, *McCall's*, Dr. Lee Salk answers a question about a mother going away to work. He warns about the dangers of leaving a child in someone else's care all day. "The type of child who seems able to develop a greater capacity for deep, warm relationships is the child who is in closer contact with the people who brought him into the world and are strongly motivated to meet his particular needs." He continues in the same vein, "I have seen too many adult patients with substantial emotional problems who have never forgotten the lonely feeling and lack of self-importance that came from returning at the end of a school day and finding no concerned parent there to greet them." [19]

Paradoxically, just when mothers are leaving the home in greater and greater numbers, the need for them to stay with their children has never been greater. We no longer have the benefit of tightly knit, fairly homogeneous communities in which certain values were tacitly understood to be shared.

In communities of yesteryear, everyone agreed that children were to act in a certain way; and if a child got out of line someone would set him straight, even though that someone was not necessarily one of his parents. The whole community shared, in a sense, in raising the community's children. Sometimes this was done merely by the strong pressure on children (and adults) to conform to certain standards of behavior.

Today it is a rare community that offers parents this kind of support. In many cases, perhaps most, even the children's grandparents, aunts, uncles, and other relatives do not live nearby to give support to the parents and a measure of emotional security to the children. There is only the immediate family for instilling values and giving emotional support. When the mother also leaves for the greater part of the day, the child is bereft.

In contrast to the pressure that used to come from the community which was based on the values of the adults, the pressure which is strongest on most children today is that of their peers—the other children. Obviously this cannot give us any help. In many cases it adds tremendously to the parents' difficulties. If a mother is gone from her child for a large part of the day, she is likely to lose her influence in favor of the peer group, which is constant.

Television is another modern influence on children. We are all horrified when we read statistics citing the great number of hours the average child watches in a week. Although there are a few good, even excellent programs for children, most of what they watch is mediocre or downright harmful. Violence is portrayed as a way of life, dishonesty and intrigue are applauded, and a totally false set of values is set forth. The influence of parents must be strong, both to strictly monitor what the children watch, and to be constantly exerting their influence, setting forth their values.

The November, 1971, *Family Circle* contains an interesting little item about women and outside jobs. It seems that in Czechoslovakia, where 70 percent of the women work outside their homes, they are very unhappy about the situation. "... while American Women's Libbers talk about day-care centers and working, the Czech women would gladly pick up their children from the state-run nursery and spend more time together at home!" [20]

Women Who Are Not Called to Be Full-Time Homemakers

There are a number of women whose calling is not to stay home, of course. There are many widows who must hold down outside jobs to support their families.

Even though they might wish to be home with their children, these women have no choice. But the emotional toll on their children is not nearly as great, because the children know that their mother is not choosing to leave them. There may still be problems, but they are not as acute as in a situation where the mother is simply pursuing another career because she prefers it to homemaking.

Then there are those who never had children or whose children have grown up and left home. God may call them to another career in which they can make a significant contribution. (On the other hand, if they feel called to use their talents as homemakers in the community, there should be no pressure on them to find another career!)

Teenagers Still Need Us

I purposely did not say "those whose children are all in school" or "those whose children are teenagers." I have known far too many children and teenagers who have skipped school and done things at home, while mother was at work, that would appall and possibly frighten their parents. There are girls who regularly skip school and entertain their boyfriends alone in the house. There is one girl I know of who is having sexual intercourse with her boyfriend at her house while her mother is at work. Her mother has no idea that this is going on, and would be most shocked and upset if she knew. This is an extreme case, but by no means rare.

Even if our children would not succumb to temptations such as these, they still need their mothers. I find that my teenagers need as much of my time as my younger children, and sometimes more. There are so many problems they need to discuss with me, so much counsel and encouragement that they need. So many of their problems are seen to be much larger than life. Often very small difficulties loom as great emergencies. As one mother of teenagers put it, "Instead of living from day to day, we live from crisis to crisis." How true. And our children need us in these "crises." Also, as their own ministries develop and grow, our role of discipler is greatly expanded.

What If—

Let us imagine, for a moment, a world in which all the thousands of wives and mothers who work outside the home suddenly quit. Unemployment would be less of a problem. The gross national product would not be nearly as gross. There would be immediate gains in ecology, and a simpler life. We would be consuming less; industry would produce less and pollute less. "Keeping up with the Joneses" would not be able to proceed as rapidly, nor would inflation be able to gallop at its accustomed pace. There would be more joy and less tension, as husbands and wives between them would be absorbing the tensions from one job. We would have more time for people, less occupation with things. It does give one pause, does it not?

A Matter of Values

Perhaps the crux of the matter is what our values are. In an article "What Every Mother Owes Her Child and Herself" from the June, 1966 *Ladies Home Journal*, Lois Benjamin and Arthur Henly talk about mothers with outside jobs whose children take care of themselves after school because they do not have access to child-care centers. They cite the case of Mrs. Andrews, from Detroit, Michigan, the mother of three boys, ages nine, seven and six. "She is an attractive woman, but looks far older than her 32 years. She has been forever *striving to reach the middle income bracket*—and never quite reaching it (italics mine). The disappointment is showing. But there is no mistaking her devotion to her children. 'My kids come first,' she says, softly but firmly.

'Much as I hated to leave them, I just had to. We needed the money more.' " [21]

The authors do not seem to recognize this bit of double-talk. The woman says her children come first, but obviously it is the middle-income bracket that comes first. She is willing to risk their welfare and safety (one day at their unsupervised play all three were seriously burned) for a second income. In effect, she is sacrificing her children for luxuries.

Most of us in the United States and Canada simply assume that television sets, automobiles, automatic washers and driers, many changes of clothes and the various other paraphernalia with which we surround ourselves are necessities. When we are honest with ourselves, we know that this is not so. When God gives us these things, we should thankfully enjoy them to the full. But they should not take priority in our lives.

The Need for Inner Resources

It does take a certain amount of inner resources to make a success of homemaking. In many ways it is easier to leave the house for a job where the boss figures out what has to be done—where there are nicely prescribed limits.

In an article entitled "Does Women's Liberation Make You Feel Inferior?" in the July, 1972 *Family Circle*, Lyn Tornabene talks about this. "A housewife's work week contains seven days that can stretch from seven in the morning until 11 at night—like an artist's or a novelist's—and there are terrible hazards in that kind of flexibility. Behavioral scientists have clearly demonstrated that humans need order in their lives to function at their best. The order of our days in many ways gives us our images of ourselves. Women whose jobs at home won't ever be nine-to-five face the endless possibility of chaotic days with sloppy endings. Their self-image is potentially a blur, and their self-esteem is in constant jeopardy. They are sitting ducks for pressure to become gainfully employed."

She goes on to tell about a psychiatrist of her acquaintance who is dispensing jobs for his women patients the way internists dispense aspirin. It is something he prescribes as a palliative—it does not cure the disease any more than aspirin does. She concludes, ". . . women who do not *have* to work must cherish that option for the privilege it is . . . those who don't want (outside) jobs but feel diminished at home need help finding a way to re-define themselves at home. Inner resources are being abandoned these days in favor of outer ones, and that, I believe, is bad."

Mrs. Tornabene has the insight and courage to say something that badly needs saying. If we cannot perform our work and find meaning in our lives without having someone else set our goals and define the limits of our jobs for us, we are in very bad shape indeed.

There is no more reason for a woman of intelligence and education to "go stale" in homemaking than in any other profession. As in most careers, she can put forth a minimum of effort and reap a minimum of reward, or she can give it all of her skill and imagination and grow accordingly.

I hold no brief for women with college degrees who limit their efforts to the narrow world of diapers and dishes and then complain that they are bored. A teacher does not think of herself merely as a corrector of tests. A pastor does not define his job in terms of the paperwork and trivial details that must be attended to. Neither may the homemaker think of herself only in terms of her chores. If she does, she will be operating only on that level. Sadly enough it is possible to be a homemaker on that level for one's whole life, just as there are some teachers who do little more than give assignments and correct tests, and some pastors who major in paperwork and details.

However, the teacher and the pastor will be more easily detected, since they usually have superiors who are responsible for seeing that they do their jobs. The homemaker, on the other hand, must depend upon her own self-discipline. There are no outside pressures from the job market—no bright young graduates waiting to be hired for her job. So she must possess inner resources of her own in order to work up to her potential.

Joel Nederhood discusses this problem in *The Holy Triangle*: "There is nothing wrong, of course, in mothers working outside the home under certain circumstances. . . . But it is ridiculous to suggest that this is necessary because a mother's work within the home is meaningless and dull. Isn't it true that many women flee their homes because the high calling of motherhood is just too much for them? It demands resources which they simply do not have. And they do not have the resources necessary because they have never looked at their tasks in the light of the Bible and asked God for the wisdom and the strength and the victory He alone can give." [22]

The Paradox of the Gospel

Fulfillment, like happiness, is as elusive as a will-o'-the-wisp when pursued. In Matthew 16:24 and 25 Jesus tells us, "If anyone wishes to be a follower of mine, he must leave self behind; he must take up his cross and come with me. Whoever cares for his own safety is lost; but if a man will let himself be lost for my sake he will find his true self."

If we homemakers are asking God to give us the resources we need, we will be able to "deny ourselves," as one translation puts it—to "leave self behind" and follow Jesus. For the gospel is not for those who are trying to fulfill themselves, carve out a niche for themselves, or find work which "meets their needs." The gospel is for those who are willing to do just the opposite. In *The God-Players*, Earl Jabay writes, "This is the strange paradox of the Gospel. We live by dying. We win by losing. We are saved by perishing. We triumph by surrendering. We come in first when we are last."

CHAPTER THIRTEEN

The Challenge for Christians

Homemaking's Broad Scope

Recently a church paper printed a letter from a woman who signed herself "A home-bound mother who is thinking about a part-time job." She wrote that while some women are completely happy to "clean, scrub, knit, bake . . . another type of mother is finished working about ten o'clock in the morning. She becomes bored. Perhaps she may go to friends for coffee (often, a bit of gossiping results). She may go shopping and spend too much money."

We have seen that the profession of homemaking is a great deal larger than the set of chores by which this woman defines it. These chores are only the beginning. After they are done we have time to raise our children the way God has commanded us in His Word, to practice hospitality, to give our talents to help those who are in need, to share our faith and make disciples. We can be enriching our minds and stretching our imaginations through literature. We can be keeping up on current events. (I have noticed that in mixed gatherings, it is usually the homemakers who are the most knowledgeable about the latest books. Their sisters with outside jobs don't seem to get time to read.) Even those who advocate outside jobs for women admit this.

In an article from the March, 1972 *McCalls'* by Felice Schwartz, Margaret Schifter, and Susan Gillotti entitled, "How to Go to Work When Your Husband Is Against It, Your children Aren't Old Enough, and There's Nothing You Can Do Anyhow" from the book by the same title, the authors are, as the title would suggest, trying to challenge women to leave their homes even when it does not seem feasible. In listing the homemaker's assets for job-hunting they write, "You've been leading a complex life, meeting demands and commitments more responsible, challenging, and maturing than you would have in most jobs. . . . You're a rare housewife indeed if you haven't kept up on cultural matters to a much greater degree than most of your office-going contemporaries." [23]

I was mentally running through a list of the books that I read in the six months before I began writing this book. It includes several of the classics, a number of novels, several books currently talked about such as *I'm OK—You're OK* by Thomas Harris, a smattering of recent books on child-raising, and several devotional volumes. Obviously if I had a regular job as a teacher (for which I was trained) besides trying to run my home and raise my children, I would not have had the time to read those books. Very likely I would have read few books other than the textbooks I would be using. The freedom and time to read, to be informed and to grow intellectually, is a tremendous bonus that comes with full-time homemaking and should not be underestimated.

The Virtuous Woman

When I first found myself in charge of a parsonage,

I was young, with two babies, and the better part of a continent between my mother and me. I had nothing but a college education and two years in Europe to prepare me for life in the middle of the prairie. We were a mile from our nearest neighbor, five and a half miles from town. The town consisted of a post office where we had to get our mail, a general store (actually a charming place), a pool hall which doubled as a barber shop, and a couple of gas stations. Our doctor was thirty-five miles away, over mostly unpaved roads. I experienced what today would be called "cultural shock."

And yet it was a growing experience for me. Looking back I can see that what helped make those years such a basically positive experience was the concern of several of the godly women in that congregation. They really cared about me. They were continually asking my husband whether I was getting along all right. But more than that, they showed their concern. I was the recipient of jars of jam, cans of honey, boxes of homemade cookies, and loaves of freshly baked bread.

During our entire four-year stay we never bought either chickens or eggs. We never had to hire a baby-sitter, either. If I wanted to accompany my husband to shop in the city for a couple of days while he was at a meeting, I had only to let one of these women know. They would gladly take care of the children for me. Although they would probably be surprised if anyone referred to them as professionals, these women are truly professional homemakers.

One woman, in particular, stands out in that community. A couple of years ago a mutual friend (a non-Christian) wrote us that this woman was "still holding the community together." What a tribute! And it is perfectly true. She *is* holding the community together. When anyone is sick, she appears with a plate of cookies. If the church has a work party organized, she is the first to come and the last to leave. When the PTA needs help in the kitchen for a supper, she will be there. When my children would go to her house for the day, I would sometimes have to persuade them to come home again.

I remember our oldest child's first birthday away from any grandparents, aunts, or uncles. This woman telephoned in the morning and asked if it would be "all right" if she and her little boy would come over for a few minutes to bring some birthday cake. She not only brought cake, but candles, ice cream, and an apron she had made as a present for our little girl. We had a fine party, complete with snapshots which she took and presented to us later.

She seems to possess a kind of spiritual radar. She senses when someone is in need of comfort or a bit of cheering up, and she is there. She has never considered whether she is "fulfilled" or "liberated." She is simply doing what God wants her to do. And she radiates happiness.

Homemaker's Very Special Contribution

In recent years women have proved that they can succeed in almost any field that was previously considered to be for men only. There are now women who are successful as doctors, lawyers, engineers, and in various other careers which had previously been virtually closed to women. No one should really be surprised that these women are doing so well. Certainly we women are not surprised. There have been (and perhaps always will be) some men who think, or at least pretend to think, that women are inferior beings. Unfortunately, there have also been some women who believed what these men told them about themselves. However, this group is rapidly diminishing. I think that most of us have known all along that we are as intelligent and capable as men. Except for the jobs requiring physical strength, there is probably no "man's" job that a woman could not handle, and handle well.

But there is one profession that is uniquely ours. In *Sixpence in Her Shoe*, Phyllis McGinley writes, "Talk as the pundits will about our contribution to industry or the sciences or the arts (and the air is noisy with their talk), it is as mothers and wives and householders that we make our unique contribution to humanity . . . the home is the world's end and its beginning—and . . . only women can properly create it." [24]

The thing that is so important for us to keep before us is that *if we choose not to do this very special job, it will simply not get done.* The mothering, the nurturing, the comforting and caring that fills the committed home-maker's day will simply be lost, and society will be impoverished. Children will not get the spiritual guidance they need. Lonely teenagers will not be listened to. Many people with problems will not be ministered to, many sick folk will go unvisited. A special human quality will disappear from our culture.

Women can give up their jobs as clerks, engineers, salespeople, doctors—other people will step in and the world will go on as smoothly as before. It will be business as usual. The groceries will still be sold, trucks loaded with merchandise will still roll across our highways, and Wall Street will carry on. Not so with homemaking. We are the special people into whose hands the homes of the country and the world have been entrusted. When we leave *this* job the world does not go on as before. It falters and begins to lose its way. We homemakers are indispensable.

Homemaking is much more than a job—it is a profession: a profession which is venerable, honorable, and of the highest benefit to mankind. We must not forget this, even though we are not receiving a paycheck for services rendered. Let us hope that we have not become so crass that we can judge the worth of an occupation only in economic terms! We must be conscious of our calling before God and the tremendous contribution that we are making to His Kingdom in our chosen role as homemakers. In the words of Phyllis McGinley, "Let none persuade us differently, or the world is lost indeed." [25]

Appendix

Notes

Appendix

Some Special Recipes

Here are some of the recipes I find indispensable. Some are family traditions, some are my own inventions, others were given to me by friends. All of them have one of two qualifications: either they are very simple but satisfying, or they are a little more work but luscious and worth the trouble. None requires complicated preparation.

SPLIT PEA SOUP

A ham bone
One package (one pound) split peas
One large onion, minced
A sliced German or Polish sausage, if your ham bone has very little meat on it
3 quarts water
Put ingredients in soup pot. Bring to a boil, then simmer 3 to 4 hours, stirring occasionally. Add salt and pepper if needed. Remove bone and laddle into bowls. Serve as a main course with hot muffins or corn bread and carrot sticks. Serves 5 or 6.

VEGETABLE & BEEF SOUP

2 pounds beef shank
1-3 pounds marrow bones—the more the better
3-6 carrots, sliced
3 stalks celery, sliced, including tops
1 bunch green onions, sliced, including tops
1 or 2 cloves garlic, cut fine
1 medium onion, chopped
1-2 teaspoons dried parsley
A large dash cloves
1/2 teaspoon celery seed
A dash lemon juice
1 can tomato soup (or several fresh tomatoes in season)
Leftover gravy (or package of gravy mix)
Any juice from cooking vegetables
Seasoned pepper and salt to taste
Optional—1/2 small green cabbage, cut up

Cover with water, bring to a boil and simmer at least 4 hours. Skim off excess fat, discard bones, cut meat in pieces. At least 15 minutes before serving add any leftover vegetables, potatoes, rice, etc. Serves 5 or 6.

MY MOTHER'S CHILI

1 1/2 pounds ground beef
2 cloves garlic, minced
A large onion, chopped
2 green peppers, chopped (1 will do when they are very expensive)
2 cans tomato soup
3 cans kidney beans (or 1 pound dried red beans, soaked overnight & then cooked)
Chili powder to taste (1 teaspoon to 2 tablespoons)
Salt & pepper to taste
Optional—1 teaspoon cumin

Put first four ingredients in large skillet and cook, uncovered, until meat is brown and vegetables are soft. If meat is very dry, add a bit of bacon fat or cooking oil. Add tomato soup and beans. Simmer at least an hour or until it thickens. Two or three hours of simmering is better.

174

HOT CHICKEN SALAD

2 full cups diced, cooked chicken
1 1/2 cups diced celery
1/2 cup sliced almonds
1 scant cup mayonnaise or Miracle Whip
1/2 teaspoon salt (scant)
1 1/2 tablespoons grated onion or 1 1/2 teaspoons dry onion
2 tablespoons lemon juice
Heat the above in a sauce pan over very low heat until heated through. Put in casserole. Cover with:
1 cup shredded Velveeta cheese
1 cup crushed potato chips
Bake at 400 degrees until hot or until cheese is melted. Celery will be crunchy. This can be cut in squares. Serves 6.

CHICKEN RICE CASSEROLE

3/4 stick of margarine
1 can each: cream of chicken soup, cream of celery soup, cream of mushroom soup, chicken gumbo soup
1 2/3 cups uncooked rice (brown, preferably)
4-5 pounds chicken parts
1 1/2 cups milk
1 teaspoon dried onion
1/4 cup diced green pepper
A dash of dried parsley
1 teaspoon poultry seasoning
Optional—1 cup blanched, slivered almonds
Melt margarine in large roaster. Add and mix together all of the soup and seasonings. Sprinkle the rice over the soup. Do not stir. Put chicken parts on top of rice. Pour the milk over all. Chicken may be sprinkled with paprika for added color. Bake uncovered at 350 degrees for 2 hours. Serves 8.

TUNA SALAD

2 cans tuna fish, drained
2-4 stalks celery, diced

1/4-1/2 head of lettuce, torn in small pieces
1 teaspoon dried onion
1 tablespoon lemon juice
Enough mayonnaise or Miracle Whip to moisten
Salt to taste
This basic recipe can be used with cooked chicken, turkey, shrimp, etc., in place of tuna fish. When using shrimp, add a dash of horseradish and serve on pineapple rings. Serves 6 or 7.

GREEN SALAD

1 package lime-flavored gelatin
1 cucumber, diced
1 small can crushed pineapple, drained (but save the juice)
Dash of lemon juice
Prepare gelatin according to directions, except use 1 cup boiling water, and the pineapple juice and lemon juice plus cold water to make 3/4 cup. When gelatin is starting to set, fold in the pineapple and cucumber. I make this in an 8-inch square pan and cut it in squares to serve.

ORANGE SALAD

This is the same as the Green Salad except you use orange gelatin instead of lime and a small can of mandarin oranges in place of the cucumber. One or two sliced bananas can be added if desired.

FESTIVE CRANBERRY MOLD

This is one of my favorite cranberry molds. It is much less work than the fresh relish type which must be put through the food chopper. It is perfect for Thanksgiving or Christmas dinner, and is a nice addition to any meal that includes poultry or ham.
1 package fresh cranberries
1 cup water
1 1/2 cups sugar
1 package lemon gelatin

12 marshmallows
1 cup celery, cut up
1 cup walnuts, cut up
Put first three ingredients in large saucepan. Bring to a boil and cook on medium heat, uncovered, until cranberries are mushy. Remove from heat, add gelatin and marshmallows. Stir until the marshmallows dissolve. Cool. Add celery and walnuts. Pour into greased mold. This makes a large ring.

GRAHAM GEMS

2/3 cup brown sugar
1 stick margarine
1 egg
1 cup sour milk
1 small teaspoon baking soda
2 cups stone ground whole wheat (graham) flour
Blend sugar and margarine, stir in egg. Add other ingredients. Fill muffin cups 2/3 full. Bake at 375°-400° for 15 minutes. Makes 12.
Before spooning into muffin cups you can add 1 cup of any of the following: raisins, chopped nuts, chopped dates, chopped dried apricots, diced apple pieces, etc. Mostly I make them plain and eat them with butter and cheddar cheese for breakfast. If you preheat your oven immediately, you can be serving these a half hour after getting the recipe out.

RICH REFRIGERATOR CHEESECAKE

When you want an elegant dessert but time is limited, stir up this simple recipe. Less trouble than baked cheesecakes, it is fully as rich and delicious.
1 can sweetened condensed milk (Eagle Brand)
1/3 cup lemon juice
1 package (8 ounce) cream cheese, softened
1 8-inch graham cracker crust (recipe on graham cracker box)
Put sweetened condensed milk in bowl, stir in lemon juice until mixture thickens somewhat. With rotary beater blend in cheese until mixture is smooth. Pour into graham cracker crust.

Chill 2 to 3 hours or until firm. If desired, top with blueberry or cherry pie filling or drained, crushed pineapple just before serving.

AUNTY PAUL'S PIE

This is a delicious memory from my childhood.

1 can sweetened condensed milk
1/3 cup lemon juice
1 can fruit cocktail, well drained (use paper toweling)
3 bananas, sliced
1 8-inch graham cracker crust

In a large bowl, stir lemon juice into sweetened condensed milk until mixture thickens somewhat. Fold in fruit cocktail and bananas. Pour into crumb crust, reserving a few crumbs to sprinkle on top. Chill 2-3 hours or until firm. Serve with whipped cream. A marachino cherry half on each serving is a nice touch.

CHOCOLATE CHEESECAKE

Rich, creamy, a chocolate lover's delight. This is a very special dessert. Since it is so rich, be sure to have plenty of coffee to accompany it.

CRUST

1 8-ounce package chocolate wafers
1/3 cup melted margarine
1/4 cup sugar
1/4 teaspoon nutmeg

Crush wafers with rolling pin. Combine crumbs, melted margarine, sugar and nutmeg in bowl; mix well. Press evenly over bottom and side (1 inch from top) of 9-inch, spring-form pan. Refrigerate.

FILLING

3 eggs
1 cup sugar
3 8-ounce packages cream cheese, softened
2 6-ounce packages chocolate chips, melted
1/8 teaspoon salt

178

1 teaspoon vanilla
1 cup commercial sour cream
In a large bowl beat eggs and 1 cup sugar with electric mixer at high speed until light. Beat in cream cheese until smooth. Add melted chocolate, vanilla, salt, and sour cream; beat well until smooth. Turn into crumb crust. Bake one hour, or until just firm when pan is shaken gently. Cool in pan on wire rack; then refrigerate, covered, overnight. Serve with lots of sweetened whip cream. Serves 16.

EASY APPLE CRISP

5 cups sliced apples
1 teaspoon cinnamon
1/2 cup sugar
Mix the above in baking pan. Then mix together:
1/2 cup butter
1/4 cup brown sugar
Add 1 cup flour. Mix with fork until mixture resembles coarse meal. Pat on top of apple mixture. Bake at 325 degrees for 45-55 minutes.
This is my favorite topping for crisp and can be used on any fruit pie filling mixture.

RHUBARB RAISIN PIE (9 inch)

CRUST

2 scant cups flour (no need to sift)
1 teaspoon salt
2/3 cup lard (no substitute)
4 tablespoons water
Cut lard into the flour and salt mixture until mixture looks like meal. Sprinkle with the water. Press into a ball. Divide in half and roll out.

FILLING

5 cups cut-up rhubarb
3/4 cup raisins
1 1/4-1 2/3 cups sugar
1/4 teaspoon almond extract

Dash of cinnamon
6 tablespoons flour
Dot with a heaping tablespoon butter
Bake at 425° for 40-50 minutes

MY GOLDEN FRUITCAKE

Apricots give this cake the special flavor that makes it distinctively different from other fruitcakes.

1 cup margarine, softened
2 cups brown sugar
4 eggs
3 scant cups unsifted flour
1 teaspoon baking powder
1 teaspoon salt
1 cup milk
1 teaspoon vanilla extract
1/2 teaspoon lemon extract
1/2 teaspoon almond extract
1 pound candied red cherries, halved
1 pound candied pineapple, cut up
2 full cups pecan halves
2 cups dried apricots, pressed tightly into cup, then cut in thirds
1 package (15 ounce) golden raisins

Prepare two 9x5x3 inch loaf pans by greasing, lining with waxed paper and greasing again. Cream margarine and sugar, stir in eggs. Add dry ingredients and milk alternately until all is mixed in. Stir in flavorings. Mix in fruit and nuts. Turn batter into pans—they will be nearly full. Bake at 250° to 275° for 2-3 hours, covering with paper the last hour. If any raisins are uncovered on top of the cakes, they may burn. After baking simply pull them out with a toothpick and discard them. When almost cool, wrap in tinfoil, then plastic bags, and refrigerate. If kept airtight they can be stored two or three months. If you use pans of half the size, subtract a half an hour from baking time.

OATMEAL SHORTBREAD

Here is a cooky recipe that gives the most for the least. It is so quick and so good.

1 cup margarine, softened
2/3 cup light brown sugar
1 1/2 cups unsifted flour
2/3 cup quick oats

Cream sugar and margarine, add flour and oats. When well mixed, press firmly and evenly into a lightly buttered cooky sheet (10x15). Bake at 300 degrees for 20-30 minutes. Cut into squares immediately, then cool in pan.

AUNTY CATHERINE'S OATMEAL COOKIES

These are the best oatmeal cookies I have ever tasted. They are great as is, but you can add nuts or chocolate chips to the batter if you like.

1 cup granulated sugar
1 cup brown sugar
1 cup lard or other shortening
1 egg
2 tablespoons cream (milk will do if you have no cream)
1 1/2 cups unsifted flour
1 heaping teaspoon soda
2 cups quick oats
1 teaspoon cinnamon
1 teaspoon each allspice and cloves

Cream sugar and shortening, mix in egg and cream. Add dry ingredients and mix well. Drop by spoonfuls onto lightly greased cooky sheet. Bake at 350 degrees for 7-9 minutes.

MISCELLANEOUS HINTS

Powdered milk can be used almost anytime a recipe calls for milk. In many cases, you need not reconstitute it before using. When preparing mashed potatoes, for instance, use the cooking water, which is hot, and simply add some powdered milk. It is not necessary to measure the milk exactly for meat loaves, either.

Cook a small pork roast and a small beef roast together for a change. Round steak and pork steak also go well together. The juices blend so that the round steak is less dry, and the gravy is delicious.

If cheese becomes old and dry, grate it on top of casseroles, meat loaves, or hamburgers.

When green peppers are plentiful, dice them and freeze them in individual plastic bags for use in cooking during the winter.

Never waste anything:

Fruit juices can go into gelatin salads or be used to make a sauce for cake or ice cream.

Stale bread can be used for french toast, crumbled into meat loaf, or made into croutons.

Juices from vegetables can go into soups or gravies.

Here is a good way to use leftovers:

In a skillet heat leftover gravy to a boil (add a package of gravy mix if you do not have enough). Add cooked potatoes, cut up; cooked meat, cut up (roast, chops, meat loaf, or any combination of these); and any or several of these leftover vegetables: cut beans, peas, carrots, corn, lima beans. Season with dried onion and chili powder. When all is heated through, sprinkle with shredded cheddar cheese. Cover for a minute or two until cheese melts. Serve with no apologies to anyone.

Notes

1. *The Expositor's Greek Testament*, edited by W. Robertson Nicoll (Wm. B. Eerdmans Publishing Co.). Used by permission.
2. *The New International Commentary on the New Testament*, by Herman Ridderbos (Wm. B. Eerdmans Publishing Co.). Used by permission.
3. *Hidden Art*, by Edith Schaeffer (Tyndale House Publishers), p. 153.
4. *The I Hate to Housekeep Book*, by Peg Bracken (Harcourt Brace Jovanovich, Inc.).
5. "Counseling," from *The Banner*, official publication of the Christian Reformed Church. Used by permission.
6. *Competent to Counsel*, by Jay E. Adams (Grand Rapids, Michigan: Baker Book House, copyright ᶜ 1970), p. 29.
7. *Ibid.*, p. 20.
8. *Ibid.*, p. 41.
9. *The Holy Triangle*, by Joel Nederhood (Grand Rapids, Michigan: Baker Book House, copyright ᶜ 1972), p. 106.
10. *Ibid.*, p. 90.
11. *The Biblical Basis for Infant Baptism*, by Dwight Henry Small (reprint; Grand Rapids, Michigan: Baker Book House, 1968), p. 45.
12. *The Art of Loving*, by Erich Fromm (Harper and Row, Publishers, Inc., p. 47.
13. *I'm OK—You're OK*, by Thomas Harris (Harper and Row, Publishers, Inc.), p. 41.

14. *The Biblical Basis for Christian Involvement in Social Concerns*, by Douglas Stuart. Evangelical Committee for Urban Ministries in Boston (ECUMB), 383 Sawmut Avenue, Boston, Mass. 02118.
15. Taken from *How to Give Away Your Faith*, by Paul E. Little. Copyright © 1962 by Inter-Varsity Christian Fellowship. Used by permission of Inter-Varsity Press, Downers Grove, Ill.
16. *With the Holy Spirit and with Fire*, by Samuel M. Shoemaker (Harper and Row, Publishers, Inc.), p. 40.
17. From an article in August, 1972, *McCalls*. Used by permission.
18. *Should Mothers Work?*, by Louise Bates Ames, in April, 1972, *Family Circle*. Used by permission.
19. From an article in October, 1972, *McCalls*. Used by permission.
20. From an article in November, 1971, *Family Circle*. Used by permission.
21. Copyright © 1966 Downe Publishing, Inc. Reprinted by permission of *Ladies' Home Journal*.
22. *The Holy Triangle*, by Joel Nederhood (Grand Rapids, Michigan: Baker Book House, copyright 1972), pp. 65, 66.
23. *How to Go to Work When Your Husband Is Against It, Your Children Aren't Old Enough, and There's Nothing You Can Do Anyhow*, by Felice Schwartz, Margaret Schifter, and Susan Gillotti, quoted in an article in March, 1972, *McCalls*. Used by permission.
24. *Sixpence in Her Shoe.* By Phyllis McGinley (Macmillan Publishing Co., Inc.). Copyright © 1960, 1962, 1963, 1964 by Phyllis McGinley.
25. *Ibid.*